STRANGE GODS

"Elizabeth Scalia masterfully presents insights in regard to the first, and yet most frequently unobserved, of all the commandments: You shall have no other gods other than the one, true God. This book provides an important message for the culture and is a must-read for all who seek the Lord in spirit and in truth."

Rev. Robert Barron
Founder of Word on Fire Catholic Ministries

"Provocative, insightful, bold, inspiring, and faith-filled, Elizabeth Scalia's musings as 'The Anchoress' never fail to gain wide readership among Catholics of every stripe. She is committed to her faith, to her church, and to God. She uses her considerable talents to share these commitments, and her joy in being Catholic, with others—online and now in print."

James Martin, S.J.
Author of *The Jesuit Guide to (Almost) Everything*

"*Strange Gods* will leave you shocked by just how many things you've turned into idols, and inspired to turn back to the only one who is really worthy of our worship. Thank you to Elizabeth Scalia for a much-needed wake-up call."

Jennifer Fulwiler
Blogger at *Conversion Diary*

"Creation is supposed to be sacramental: a window into and a rumor of the glory of God. But precisely because it's so beautiful, we can make the mistake of worshipping and serving created things instead of the Creator. We are like children who want the box and throw away the present on Christmas morning. Elizabeth Scalia shows us how to find the love and peace we've always really wanted by turning away from idols to the living God made fully manifest in Jesus Christ."

Mark P. Shea
Author of *The Heart of Catholic Prayer*

"In her important and courageous new book, *Strange Gods*, Elizabeth Scalia presents us with a truth we avoid at our own peril: four thousand years after Yahweh declared, 'You shall have no other gods before me,' our own idol-making far outstrips that of the ancient world. A fascinating perspective on one of the most urgent spiritual problems of our era."

Paula Huston
Author of *Simplifying the Soul*

"Elizabeth Scalia is a true post-modern anchoress, writing with honesty what she has learned of God's mystery from within her digital cell. *Strange Gods* is a meditation on a perennial truth: all of us face the temptation of confusing God with our selves. Like her medieval ancestors in faith, this anchoress sees through the distractions that ensnare us, and invites us to refocus our desire on what is most lasting— a rich, broad, deep understanding of love, and an equally rich, broad, and deep probing into the mystery of God."

Tim Muldoon
Coauthor of *Into the Deep*

"Elizabeth Scalia showed me just how many unrecognized 'little idols' I have that shove God further out of reach. It isn't because he has moved away, as she points out, but because I can't have a meaningful conversation if I'm only willing to talk to myself in the mirror about how wonderful I am. If for no other reason, you need this book to contemplate her focus on the Beatitudes, which was a wake-up call on how to apply that central piece of Scripture to my own life. This book is a keeper so I can reread it when I need to remember how the cross shatters the snares that bind me."

Julie Davis
Author of *Happy Catholic*

"We need to be challenged by one of our own, someone who knows by experience that we are opinionated, noisy, cluttered, and busy in our homes and offices. Someone who knows our offices are often in our homes and, who relates to how easily distracted we are by chimes, buzzers, beeps, chirps, ringtones, pings, and other alerts that mean someone is trying to reach us. We need someone who knows how quickly we respond to those distractions with riveted attention, and how uncomfortable we are with silence. Elizabeth Scalia is that someone. She offers an alert that someone is indeed trying to reach us, but in the still small voice we don't hear while hitting the refresh tab and checking social media inboxes, eager for the next message. Elizabeth Scalia knows—and characteristically nails it with irresistible appeal because she says it colorfully and well—what we know and what we haven't yet figured out. We need pithy messages. This is pithy: God still runs the ultimate social network and the commandments still rule—and the first two contain them all. The key is Love, which is inexpressibly beyond 'Like.'

And it constitutes the only comfort zone we can know in the human network, and the only connection we'll ever need to the eternal."

Sheila Liaugminas
Host of *A Closer Look* and Network News Director
Relevant Radio

"Today, there are many 'Caesars' who demand your allegiance: technology, money, sex, and power. So how can we resist? Elizabeth Scalia shows the way in *Strange Gods*: a clear, intelligent guide for those radicals who want to subvert these false lords and instead bow to the one true God."

Brandon Vogt
Author of *The Church and New Media*

"In this worthy meditation, super-blogger Elizabeth Scalia posits that the strangest false god of all is the god we make of ourselves. She shows us the ways we become enslaved and ensnared. She guides us to more fully surrender in prayer. She reflects on the difficult but essential task of detaching with love."

Heather King
Author of *Shirt of Flame*

STRANGEGODS

Unmasking the Idols in Everyday Life

Elizabeth Scalia

The Anchoress at Patheos.com

ave maria press AmP notre dame, indiana

Founded in 1865, Ave Maria Press is a ministry of the United States Province of Holy Cross.

www.avemariapress.com

Paperback: ISBN-10 1-59471-342-1, ISBN-13 978-1-59471-342-2

E-book: ISBN-10 1-59471-357-X, ISBN-13 978-1-59471-357-6

Cover window © iStockphoto.

Cover and text design by John R. Carson.

Printed and bound in the United States of America.

Library of Congress Cataloging-in-Publication Data
Scalia, Elizabeth.
  Strange gods : unmasking the idols in everyday life / Elizabeth Scalia.
    pages cm
  Includes bibliographical references.
  ISBN 978-1-59471-342-2 (pbk.) -- ISBN 1-59471-342-1 (pbk.)
  1. Idolatry. I. Title.
  BV4627.I34S23 2013
  241--dc23
                              2012045730

★ ★ ★

To Pat

"The pedestal with my name on it."

★ ★ ★

Contents

Acknowledgments

Thanks to my editor, Patrick McGowan, who suffered through the process of my writing this while I was constantly distracted with an overcrowded schedule and what I have discovered to be a very short attention span. I would have dedicated the book to you, but my husband's sufferings were much, much greater than yours, if you can imagine it. So he deserves the dedication.

Thanks to Father Robert Barron, Mark Shea, Brandon Vogt, Heather King, James Martin, S.J., Jennifer Fulwiler, Paula Huston, Julie Davis, Tim Muldoon, and Sheila Liaugminas (what impressive company for a peasant like me). All of you were generous enough, trusting enough, and daring enough to recommend this book while having only an incomplete product to read. I hope and pray I have not embarrassed any of you and that none of you will be reduced to saying, "Well, I don't always agree with her, but sometimes her snout finds an acorn."

Thanks to all of the people at Patheos.com, from the big kahunai I answer to, to the support staff, IT folk, designers; and thanks to the newest additions to the Catholic Channel who cheerfully answer to me and never grumble. I have never worked with a better, more upbeat, professional, hardworking, and downright pleasant group of people in my life. The adventure has been, frankly, wonderful.

Thanks to Jamie and Carol for all they teach me, which is depressing because I am old enough to be their mother, but they're just that smart, ethical, and (thankfully) forgiving.

Thanks to Jack for encouraging me, making me laugh, and providing the live-music soundtrack that heartened me.

Thanks to Paul Snatchko (the *Magnificat* pulled me through more than one morning as I wrote this); Antonio Spadaro, S.J.; Monsignor Paul Tighe; Grant Gallicho; Sarah K., who calls me Miss A; and Dianne, Steve, Tom, and Pat, who have all inspired me at some point.

Thanks to Saint Philip Neri, Saint Benedict, and Mary, my mother, and John Cardinal O'Connor—who patiently taught what I resisted learning.

Thanks to all of my in-laws, who have been the source of unwavering, if puzzled, support, and to my dear Lil' Bro Thom, who must get working on a book of his own.

Pat, were it not for you, I am convinced I would not be alive today, and I certainly never would have finally found what I was looking for. You know what that is. I thank God for you every day of my life.

Introduction

It was perhaps a year or so after the 9/11 terrorist attacks, during the debate over the passage of the Patriot Act. I was reading comment threads on a right-leaning political forum and noted one woman who vociferously objected to the legislation. She was a "stalwart conservative" and a bit of a rugged individualist—she could shoot a gun and dress a kill. If I had known of Sarah Palin's existence at the time, I'd have favorably compared the two.

She feared putting too much power in the hands of government—even if it meant giving that power to a president she basically liked. Her main concern was that she fully expected these expanded powers to eventually be abused. Her patriotism, she declared, demanded that she place her concerns about liberty over issues of security and party loyalty. She wrote (and I paraphrase here): "Once people acquire power, they don't give it up at some later date, they just add to it."

Perhaps it was a measure of how disoriented the 2001 attacks had left many people, for the woman was not saying anything most conservatives would not say today about the size and scope of government. At the time, though, the rage and indignation expressed against her concerns flared up with a surprising heat. The woman was accused of being paranoid; some suggested that her rural life precluded her ability to understand the gravity of the situation; some suggested (rather cavalierly, in my view) that people with nothing to hide need not worry about a few government intrusions meant to ensure our safety and security. A few people described this woman's concern as sensible, but then added something that stuck with me. They said she ought to be able to put aside these concerns in support of a president who—wasn't it obvious?—had been put into his office by God.

For my part, I thought the concerns the woman expressed were valid, and I was completely unprepared to see this formerly popular participant quickly become unwelcome within the forum. As she was driven away, an image formed in my mind. It was an image of birds flying in unison and then suddenly dive-bombing against a nonconformist who had been deemed unfit for the formation. In a matter of weeks, she was gone, but before she left, she made a point of posting the famous quotation that is attributed to Ben Franklin: "Anyone who trades liberty for security deserves neither liberty nor security." She predicted that her compatriots would one day regret the government's overreach. She also predicted that someday they would hear candidates pledge to reduce intrusive government powers, only to see those same politicians further grow those powers once they attained their offices. This would be possible thanks to the very precedents then being cheered on.

As fascinating as that whole exchange was, what I found most striking was the ferocity of the party loyalists. Conscious of the attacks on New York and Washington and of all the ways our freedoms could be used against us, the forum participants seemed willing to ignore everything they might have previously known or believed about human nature, the human heart, and the vagaries of power. They expressed total confidence that President George W. Bush would use such heightened surveillance capabilities "only for good." It was around this time that I began to wonder whether I was witnessing a kind of idolatry.

Perhaps the strong indignation felt by most of those who posted angry comments began as a kind of patriotic projection, I thought. Many of these folks thought of the office of the president as something almost sacred, and President Bush's term was following one disgraced by sexual scandal. In Bush's tremendous respect for the job, as well as his overt religiosity, they had found a man who was not simply a political figure, but someone with whom to identify—someone whose values were of a piece with their own. Believing that they themselves would never abuse power, they assumed he wouldn't either. So what was there to worry about? With that concern settled, it did not take much imagination to begin to see the placement of "a prayerful, Christian man" in the White House during a time of political unrest as a clue to the workings of God's mind. From there it seemed almost natural to endow all of the president's moves and motives—at least for a while—with a supernatural "godly" wisdom.

Had they made an idol of Bush himself? I don't think so, and I am certain he would be horrified to think that might be the case. But I had read enough comments suggesting that he was "God's servant on earth" to make it a near thing—near enough, in any

case, to justify chasing off a woman for asking perfectly
legitimate questions.

   In the aftermath, my thoughts sometimes turned a
little cynical. I thought those who wanted to believe in
the Wizard of Oz would pay no attention to the man
behind the curtain; those who wanted to believe in the
illusion of fast-and-perfect security solutions would not
question the means of bringing them about. I began to
worry that those making such comments on the forum,
who were not bad people, were unwilling to pull back
the curtain and look deeply at a policy if it meant dis-
turbing their deepest hope: that safety, security, and
apple-pie contentment would soon be restored. Why?
In a word: anxiety. They wanted their fears quelled and
their ideas affirmed, and they were going in a dangerous direction to get the security they felt they were
entitled to. If there was idolatry going on, I suspected
that the idol was not "Dubya" himself. Nor was the
idol their hope. Rather, I decided, it was the anxiety
beneath it—lying coiled like a snake under the mist—
that the America they had known might be over. It was
in service to this strange god of anxiety—which hissed
of threats to everything familiar, sure, and safe, and
played to naturally protective instincts—that our rural
friend was chased away.

   Looking back, I wonder if that lonely contributor
had a good understanding not just of liberty but also
of worship. It often is forgotten or ignored, but the
Judeo-Christian tradition has some pretty strong things
to say about idolatry. Idols are not like opinions or
even convictions. They don't ask for consensus or even
strong advocacy—they demand worshippers. Perhaps,

drawing on her understanding of the God of Abraham and what this God had to say about human nature, she decided she would not bow to an idol of anxiety. She dared to opine that the proffered solutions would, in fact, prevent America and Americans from being quite so free, quite so unencumbered ever again, and that this loss of freedom was an affront not just to political liberty but also to the proper worship of God.

Like my forum friends—and, at the time, more than 70 percent of America—I approved of George W. Bush. My vote for him in 2000 was the first I'd ever cast for any Republican, and I sometimes surprised myself at how boisterous I could be in my defense of him in the face of what I thought of as needless and unfair jeering by some. I confess that I, too, wanted to believe that he was, somehow, a man apart from most men—that a Patriot Act in his hands was something less dicey than it would be in someone else's. But deep down, I too was a little uneasy.

When I did venture to suggest that there was, in fact, a troubling aroma of idolatry wafting within the breezy confidence of some of those commenting, I was kindly informed that—being made up of Christian believers—the forum was in no danger of falling into sin against that great commandment. God was still all; George W. Bush was simply his agent, and the two were in no danger of being confused. I was less kindly rebuffed when I went further and wondered aloud—as I have many times since over the years—whether there was a danger of political ideologies themselves, and not just people, becoming idols; and what would be required to disenthrall us if that was indeed the case.

Suffice it to say, I wasn't long for that forum. While I was never dive-bombed out of their formation like the hunting Sarah Palin prototype, my flying was considered wayward enough that I was simply ignored and left to find my own bumptious sky. But the questions raised there have lingered. On my blog, *The Anchoress*, and in various other pieces I have written in both secular and religious venues, I have occasionally ventured to suggest that the sort of ideological tribalism that informed my blue-collar, union-member parents—and inspired them to vote mostly Democrat (their aberrational support of Dwight D. Eisenhower notwithstanding)—has been supplanted by a move toward an idolatry that will brook no dissent and keeps party members prostrated in the proper direction.

My concerns about idolatry were routinely ignored, shot down, or simply jeered at by readers visiting my site until around the time of the 2008 elections, when some on the right finally found something akin to idolatry in the videos of children singing odes to Barack Obama. One saw a hint of it in *Newsweek* editor Evan Thomas's claim that Obama was "above the country, above the world, a sort of god; [he's] going to bring all different sides together."[1] Thomas took some heat for those comments and later clarified that he was not being "literal."[2]

If Thomas was unjustly harangued by those who did not see a messiah in President Obama, it was in part because the 2008 presidential campaign did offer some troublingly messianic portraits of the man. And candidate Obama, a professed Christian, did little to discourage an excessive deference that permitted neither vetting, nor criticism, nor even the japeries of late-night talk-show humor.[3] Vetting, criticism, and mockery—allowed no target in Obama—consequently came down twice as hard on John McCain's running mate, Sarah Palin. As news outlets announced they were sending teams of investigators to Wasilla, Alaska, to comb through the candidate's trash[4], the comedy writers found their foil in Palin. In reaction, Palin quickly became, for many on the far right, their untouchable and adored one—their counterpart to Obama. The more the press savaged her, the less her fans would tolerate even the mildest of constructive criticisms from sympathetic bloggers (like me). By November 2008, fifties-style partisan tribalism looked almost quaint compared to the divine illusions that were becoming attached to both candidates. I became convinced that Americans had wholly thrown themselves before two golden calves. Calves that—like the original one described in Exodus 32:1–7—were nothing but bright reflectors, showing us back to ourselves.

If God created humankind in his image, we humans tend to create gods in our own image—or perhaps more correctly, we humans create gods so reflective and shiny, they keep us looking at ourselves. In the 2008 election, I believed I was seeing precisely that in the hyperbolic support of both Barack Obama and Sarah Palin. The urbane, polished, sophisticated, and well educated looked at Obama, saw themselves, and loved him for it. Putting him in the White House meant putting themselves in there. As a Catholic priest stands "*in persona Christi*," Obama stood "*in persona meum*." For the Palin fans, her plain-speaking, hard-working,

up-from-the-middle-class story was their story, and
elitist mockery of her non-Ivy college degree and her
"you betcha" cheerfulness was a demonstration of disdain directed toward them. Voters over-identified with
whichever idol best reflected them back to themselves.
They loved the ideas they were hearing because the
ideas did not challenge but only affirmed.

There is a quotation attributed to Saint Gregory of
Nyssa: "Concepts create idols; only wonder compre-
hends anything." A simpler translation reads "ideas create idols; only wonder leads to knowing." I've come
to believe that an idol is an *idea*, fleshed out or formed
by craftiness and a certain needy self-centeredness.
The golden calf constructed by the Jews in Exodus
was a creation forged from the valued possessions of
a confused, frightened people—people who, alone in
the desert, sought something upon which they could
project the qualities they imagined in themselves. The
reflective gold gave them affirmation of their strength
and greatness, which they could confirm with their own
eyes, mirrored back at them.

While most of us today have a vague sense of when
adulation of a person or thing becomes silly or even
dangerous, we perhaps do not always truly understand
when and where (and why) we fall into worshipping
idols. When Jews and Christians think of idolatry as a
sin, the above-mentioned Exodus story quickly comes
to mind. Then, just as quickly, the story is pushed aside.
Of course *we* cannot be idolators. We are refined and
educated people. We have studied. We know our faith.
We can recite our creed. We don't live in a time in
which mere *things* are worshipped. We know that a silly

golden calf cannot be a god—at least not our god—and we dismiss the notion from our minds.

But let us, for a moment, consider the idol as the God of Moses saw it. The very first commandment of the Ten Commandments includes the phrase, "You shall not have other gods besides me" (Ex 20:3). Other translations use the phrase "you shall not have strange gods before me." Do we stop to think of what it means to have something "before God"? It means to put something "first," yes, but more fundamentally, it means to put something "in front" of God, as one might put a screen in front of a fireplace and therefore place it "before" the fire. What is before God, then, is also before us; it stands between God and us; it separates us from him. Just as a covenant of marriage cannot grow in closeness and oneness—cannot become one flesh—if something is put between a couple, the covenant between God and humanity cannot grow and survive if our strange, self-reflective idols are placed between ourselves and him.

I look at our modern mania for educational credentials as a kind of idol—a thing so burnished and glittery that sometimes the perfect candidate for a position is never seen because the required credential is hovering between him and Human Resources; and the idol—the thing that reflects our self-imaginings back to us—must be served. If a company sees itself as a bastion of certified intellectuals, it will seek out credentials that validate that idea, even if it means missing out on acquiring an autodidact in the process. In 2010, journalist Pete Hamill was awarded an honorary high-school diploma from the Jesuit-run prep school he had dropped out of fifty-nine years earlier. He had managed to build a career on the strength of his capabilities, but, as he told the *New York Times*, "It was the last period when you could do that and still have a life. Try getting a job on a newspaper, now, without the [collegiate] resume."[5] In truth, one does not need a degree to be a fine writer—but one might need one to placate the strange god of intellectual pretense.

We dismiss the golden calf story and its lessons at our peril. It's true that we are no longer literally flinging our precious metals into a crucible and buffing up stolid beasts of burden to worship. In some ways matters are worse, for we do not know the idols we bow down to. Our present-day idols are much less obvious, but they are also less distant and more ingrained within us. Idols begin with ideas. From there, we shape them in the psyche, grow them in the ego, and then engage with them intimately, throughout our lives, in our families, our culture, our entertainments, and our political discourse. We create idols out of our norms of behavior, our material possessions, and social status. We even create them out of our faith.

I intend this slim book to be the start of an adventure—a look at the myriad ways we who call ourselves "believers" and "people of faith" and who believe idolatry to be something ancient, outmoded, and outside of ourselves, are in fact everyday idolators. We are so comfortable with our idols and so convinced that they are built on entirely correct ideas that we have stopped wondering at anything and, therefore, are comprehending almost nothing.

Since I have suggested that we make idols of credentials, it is perfectly natural for you to wonder what possible expertise I am bringing to this subject, particularly as my educational background is unrelated to theology, biblical studies, religious studies, social studies, art, music, or theater. My expertise is grounded in experience, for I am a great idolator and have been all of my life. Like an ex-drunk who is the only one who can understand where you have been, where you are now, and how you can escape from a perpetual alcoholic haze, I wish to share what I know in order to assist in clearing out all the cluttering self-created deities that stand before God and before us—between us and the satisfaction of our deepest longing, which is ecstatic union with our Creator.

It is no small undertaking—because we can barely clear out an old idol before we erect a brand-spanking-new one in its place—but neither is it a dreary one. Like any good twelve-step sponsor, I aim to help you discover your idols by revealing some of mine to you. We will look at how idols block our access to God and at how convenient it is that the word *idol* begins with *i*. We will examine how ordinary, commonly accepted ideas take root and become gargantuan "godlings" that block both God and others from our sight. We will scrutinize the ways we misuse language and wrestle it to the ground, if we must, in order to make it serve our strange gods. The journey will provide warnings about the lures that are cast our way in an effort to keep us distant and distracted from the Creator and from our own lives. We will even talk about a complex, double-sided reality I call "super idolatry" that leads us directly away from everything that is good by making hate feel remarkably like love, mostly because—again—it affirms our own puny ideas.

So, welcome to an adventure of discovery that may afford you the satisfaction of some deconstruction. When my kids were little, they liked nothing better than to kick over the very blocks they had carefully, cunningly erected. We will do something like that in these pages, hopefully to great, path-clearing effect. It is my sincere wish that by identifying our idols for what they are, we can begin removing them from all the high places we have allowed them to be enshrined— before our eyes, in our hearts, between each other, and between God and us. In that way, we can begin to embrace the fullness of understanding that has been designed for us since Eden, covenanted to us through Moses and Christ, and awaits our reclamation.

CHAPTER ONE

God before Us

Whenever I get a call about a domestic dispute," a police officer told a teen group I facilitated at church, "I ask Jesus to come with me and to stand between me and the couple, and also to stand between the couple themselves."

"He is peace," the cop explained, and being peace, his presence could only make a bad or threatening situation better. He confessed further, "I've gotten into the habit of making that same prayer whenever my wife and I start arguing, or me and my kids."

The idea of asking Christ to stand between our difficulties and ourselves may seem quirky, at first. Isn't God supposed to lead us? Aren't we supposed to rely upon him to "do" for us? Well, yes and no. As Christians we believe in a God who is both infinitely above us, and, as our creator, also closer and more intimately connected to us than we are to ourselves. In times of difficulty, we do well to ask God to be *with* us, to strengthen us so that we may draw on the gifts and resources already given us.

In asking God to be with him, this police officer got specific. "Come and stand between" is another way of saying, "stand among all of these flying things teeming about in this situation: the couple's love that has become hurt, twisted, and chaotic; the ideas of espousal that have become warped and even dangerous; the anger held so dearly; the addictive need to be right. Stand among them and subdue them; stand before them in majesty so that your peace and your truth are unimpeded as we work through this difficulty." Although not an academic theologian, the cop was, in my estimation, doing theology. He was instinctively obeying God's command to the Israelites at Mount Sinai; namely, he was giving primacy to God in each situation he encountered. "You shall not have other gods besides me." This meant no gods other than the God who had freed the Israelites, yes, but it meant something deeper as well. It meant inviting God's presence—the living, breathing truth of who God is—to reside amid all of our thoughts, feelings, and actions, at all times.

To place anything—be it another deity or something more commonplace like romantic love, anger, ambition, or fear—before the Almighty is to give it preeminence in our regard. To become too attached to a thought or feeling or thing is to place it *between* God and ourselves. When we attach ourselves to something other than God, God's presence is blocked, unseen, and disconnected from our awareness. The straight line between creature and Creator is then impeded, and—as with most unwise detours—disorientation follows.

Why do people allow their relationship with God to become disoriented? Sadly, the problem usually starts with love. The human heart craves attention and love—love is the common longing of our lives. We may search for a career, or wealth, or status, but the desire to be loved and valued is usually at the root of our strivings. Finding this kind of love can be difficult. Giving love can be more difficult still. Sometimes, discouraged or impatient in our search, we chase illusions and yearn not for the give-and-take of a lifetime of sacrificial love but the fifteen minutes of fame Andy Warhol once predicted everyone would enjoy. Lacking loving relationships, we yearn instead for an audience. We're sure our allotment of attention, when it finally comes, will grow into something—that in our uniqueness we will shine with such a distinctive brightness that we will immediately be set apart from the rest of dull humanity, and love will follow.

It is not a bad thing to want to be loved; it is not a bad thing to have enough self-awareness to know who we are in the world and to desire personal excellence. Even a certain measure of ego and pride, if balanced by self-knowledge and humility, is not the worst thing. Ego and pride can push us to achieve excellence and a true sense of identity. But left unchecked or knocked out of balance, they can enslave us.

There is a great scene in the film *Moonstruck*, wherein a decent, dignified, middle-aged woman with a once loving but now unfaithful spouse finds herself eating supper in a restaurant with an attractive middle-aged man she has noticed a few times before, usually in the company of beautiful women in their late twenties. He turns out to be an English professor, and he is not without intelligence, charm, and even some decency. But he is a little vain. Worse for him, he is clearly tired of his vanity, the egotistical version of himself that he offers to the world. His vanity has led him to feeling a fraud at his work and to engaging in a series of disastrous relationships with the younger women. He is now profoundly lonely.

In their conversation, it is clear that the professor longs for something more authentic, and he instinctively senses something real in the middle-aged woman. The woman, for her part, is a little worn out from knowing that her husband, whom she loves dearly, is being unfaithful. She accepts the professor's attention— but only to a point. As he walks her home, the man wonders if the woman might invite him in. When she refuses, he assumes there are other family members to consider. "No," she says, "the house is empty. I can't invite you in because I'm married. And because I know who I am." When he attempts to elicit sympathy from her, saying he's "a little cold," she replies with perfect and friendly understanding, "You're a little boy, and you like to be bad." It's a beautiful scene that addresses our craving for love. The man is trapped by his desire to be adored and thought important—he is trapped by illusions. To a degree even he knows it, but he is still trapped. The woman, although she is hurting and not completely immune to the professor's charms, is not trapped. She knows who she is and what love is.

It is not just our own hurts and egos that create illusions, of course. Illusions are out there, constantly on sale. Images and visions offered up by advertisers can keep us recklessly careening about in search of some elusive idea of perfection. When we listen to these voices, our pride and ego are neither acknowledged nor reined in. Rather they run wild, urging that we assert ourselves, pursue the notice of others—that we control our environments and even insert ourselves into conversations and life stories that are actually none of our business. We are encouraged in this by a culture that is over-connected, media saturated, and weirdly obsessed with the fake glamour of "reality" exhibitionism.

With our vision bedazzled by our fears, insecurities, egos—and all of the pretty people paraded before us wearing all the newest clothes and owning all the latest gadgets—our distractions cease to look like pale imitations of love, but instead, become reasonable facsimiles. The fascination and admiration of others is love, isn't it? Or close enough? It must be, because we know how much we ourselves are mesmerized by our favorite iThis and eThat and how much we love our favorite artist, our favorite politician, and our favorite sports figure. We can't get enough of our favorite website or our Twitter feed.

Convinced that what has enticed us unto obsession is about love, we gather it all unto ourselves. We become encased within it until the God who is the source and giver of all love, all reality, and all truth—who actually does see how distinctly each and every one of us glows because he willed it—is hidden from view. He's like a forgotten gift, shoved to the back of a crowded mantel, which is crammed with shiny, empty things.

And yet, in those rare moments when we find ourselves alone and the gadgetry silent, we feel we are at a loss. With nothing to distract us, we come face to face with a keening emptiness. The void we thought to fill with noise and superficial friendships and tinkery things presents itself to us in a resounding echo. Silence is then terrifying, but only because it lays bare our loneliness, our self-recriminations, and our doubts. Possessing nothing that is equal to those depths, we sense the need to distract ourselves and the cycle begins to churn again.

If we are wise, we will come to recognize the illusions both within and without that attempt to trap us, and ask God to come between them and us. We will ask God to help us remember who we are. If we are foolish, God will often come to us anyway, in dramatic, not always easy-to-understand ways that force us to focus. No wonder, as my aunt used to say, "God will often write straight with crooked letters," in the learning curve of our lives.

I can say all this with such offensive certainty because I, too, create and give in to illusions every single day, as does just about everyone I know. Our shared humanity, broken since Eden, makes unwitting and constant collaborators in illusion of us all. We may take some comfort in the fact of our commonality—let's face it, all of our weaknesses seem less glaring when they are shared—but should we shrug our failings off as being mere human nature? Ought we to be so complacent about how willing we are to create illusions by the shelf-full? It's a serious question but one that our era does not take seriously—mostly because it does not recognize illusion-chasing for what it is—idolatry.

When our modern culture deigns to entertain a notion of idolatry at all, it confines the notion to a few verses of Exodus and the pop-culture excesses of teenage girls. Anyone taking seriously the question of whether we have set ourselves up for idolatry will surely be dismissed as someone unfathomably naïve, or a goofy religious fanatic, or both. What does it even mean, to put something "before God," and why would it matter to God, anyway? He's God! How insecure and needy and manipulative could God be to even make such a command?

It matters because of love—not the human love we know, which is too often so needy, insecure, and manipulative that we have no difficulty projecting these attributes on to the Creator, but the supernatural love that springs from a source that is nothing but love. "You have made us for yourself, O Lord," wrote Saint Augustine, "and our hearts are restless until they rest in you."

The command against idolatry comes early in the Ten Commandments. If we take the commandments seriously, we will recognize that, far from being a contentious list of outmoded rules, they are in fact a primary channel by which we may find that rest and peace of which Augustine speaks. The commandments may be described as "a couple of things we won't do unless we have to, followed by more things we will surely do, unless we're told in no uncertain terms that we can't."

God, understanding our self-interested natures better than we do, first sets up proper relationships: Love God, have no other gods, keep the Sabbath holy, and honor your parents. God then gives commandments meant to save us from ourselves: Don't kill, don't debase yourself or others, don't steal, don't lie or gossip, and don't covet. To modern ears—particularly those of a perpetually adolescent bent—the Ten Commandments seem a tiresome bit of parental finger wagging, an Almighty scold of no, no, no, offered to creatures inclined toward the pursuit of yes in all things.

Perhaps that is the reason the list includes the commandment to "honor thy father and thy mother," which can strike us as oddly personal and sometimes a difficult notion, to boot. Why does *that* matter? It matters because our parents are often the models and means by which we fix our notions of God—sometimes for our whole lives. If we are lucky enough to have had loving, generous parents, an exhortation to "honor" them can sound like a no-brainer. For those of us raised with difficult parental situations, however, the commandment can immediately turn us off from seeking out a trusting relationship with God. This happens most particularly if we have already made a kind of deity of our hurt and anger toward them and have grown comfortable honoring those emotions. The point is to "honor" our parents as purposeful pieces of God's plans for us, but not to make gods of them out of love or godlings from our hurt. As Rabbi Simon Jacobson explains:

> It's not about your relationship with your parents, it's about your relationship with

> your life . . . honoring your parents is like
> [God] telling you to honor the life that
> was given to you, even if your parents were
> almost incidental, or if they did everything
> possible to crush that life . . . the life is still
> there. Should you dishonor the life, you will
> become not only a victim of your parents
> but you will continue to loathe yourself and
> dishonor G-d and your own soul.[1]

Our parents are not always—or even usually—cognizant of the fact they are modeling God for us, but as children we seek from them our sustenance and our love, and if our needs are perfectly met in them, we have no particular desire to steal, kill, covet, and so forth. Unfortunately, no parent is perfect—our parents' parents weren't either—and each of us carries into our adult lives our individual voids and bare spots. We have lacked perfection since the original sin of Eden, and through millennia God has been intent on reclaiming and restoring us to himself, the source where all of our needs are truly met.

We encounter a huge part of that reclamation effort within the direct communication drawn by God and delivered by Moses, but what we seldom realize is this: all of the commandments are simply an expansion of the very first commandment—the one about gods and idols. This command is given primacy not because the Creator is insecure and in need of constant attention, but because it is the one commandment that, if obeyed, renders all of the others quite nearly moot. Were we not continually making idols of the objects of our desire—all of those shiny things we cannot resist grabbing on to—nothing would be cluttering up the space between ourselves and God; the lines would be straight and the crooked letters rendered unnecessary.

The "you shall nots" are less a list of restrictions and limitations than an invitation to keep turning back to God, who will "satisfy the desire of every living thing" (Ps 145:16). The "shall nots" say, "Don't steal that; look at me. Don't objectify her with lust; look at me. Don't nurse your anger unto death! Look at me. Do not look out there, not even to your past, be it good or bad; and do not look to your earthly desires. Look at me, and let me love you, and you will have no need of the rest."

Jesus tells us this himself in the Gospel of Matthew:

> When the Pharisees heard that he had silenced the Sadducees, they gathered together, and one of them [a scholar of the law] tested him by asking, "Teacher, which commandment in the law is the greatest?" He said to him, "You shall love the Lord, your God, with all your heart, with all your soul, and with all your mind. This is the greatest and the first commandment. The second is like it: You shall love your neighbor as yourself. The whole law and the prophets depend on these two commandments. (Mt 22:34–40)

By instructing us to look at God with love and do the same with everyone else, Jesus is telling us, "Take your eyes off yourself." God does not say, "Love me first," because God has rejection issues, and Jesus does not add, "And then love your neighbors," because he simply wants us to play well with others. These commandments are, in fact, deeply personal ones. They are meant to lead us away from those empty depths of our being where the idols are formed and polished and brought to the fore of our regard.

In his Sermon on the Mount, Christ taught that anyone who looks on another with lust has "already committed adultery" in the heart (Mt 5:28). Similarly to be filled with rage at another is already to have committed murder in the heart. I suspect this is because we attach ourselves so completely to our feelings that they easily take ownership of us. We entertain our feelings with all our heart and all our soul and all our mind. Our feelings, desires, and convictions become our gods and, exactly as strange gods are wont to do, they lead us astray, down circuitous paths that appear to be taking us somewhere but are forever leading us back into the dungeon of ourselves.

- I am so mad at you. (I feel forgotten, neglected, and betrayed.)
- I am so committed to this cause. (I find people who agree with me here and not elsewhere.)
- I want this new thing so badly. (I must not be left out.)
- I am so engaged with this argument. (I must make them think as I think.)
- I must have sex with him. (I must see myself as I want to see myself—but in his eyes, reflecting back at me.)

In the depths of our dungeons, we forge our chain links capital *I* by capital *I*. What bossy little strange gods we are! We are needy and insecure, demanding capitulation, acceptance, and even adoration from everyone in our sphere. We rebel at the notion of God handing us ten commandments; but our demands are much more numerous, and we inflict them upon everyone and then gnash the teeth when denied.

But the greatest commandment, coupled with what Jesus called "the second,"—which sum up all the rest— is meant to save us from ourselves. The commandments are meant to save us from the self-excavated pit of discontent into which we must finally fall if we cannot see these commandments for the gifts they are and use them to unbend our *I* chains, detach and become truly free.

The police officer who asked Jesus to stand between a couple and their anger and to stand between himself and their dispute would be the first to tell you he is no theologian, and yet his prayer gives evidence of keen insight. A couple in screaming turmoil are two people whose strange gods of ego, anger, insecurity, and perhaps much more have so overwhelmed them that there are no more straight, unobstructed lines between them and the God who is truth. In this case, things can very quickly devolve into chaos, which is where evil thrives. In begging Jesus to come, the cop is intercepting the swirling miasma of competing strange gods; he is creating space for reality, which resides in Christ. In asking Jesus to stand between himself and the couple, he is both seeking protection from these idols of intense feeling and displacing his own strange gods—the ones that stoke his jadedness, his experience, his fear—and he is giving primacy to the God of all, who is peace.

This is sound theology, and it is accessible. If we accept it, then a straightening out of our lives, our understanding, and our relationships with God, with others, and with ourselves is wholly in our grasp. To begin to clear the lines of communication, we need to take a look the idols that devil us in everyday life. We will begin with the most challenging idol of all—ourselves.

CHAPTER TWO

God after Us: The Idol of I

*Every evil screams out only one message:
"I am good!" And not only does it scream,
but it demands that the people cry out
tirelessly in response: "You are good, you
are freedom, you are happiness!"*

ALEXANDER SCHMEMANN

I began the first chapter by highlighting the importance of putting nothing before God, of consciously allowing nothing to come between us and the Creator who loves us into being and from whose hands, Pope Benedict XVI recently said, "we never fall."[1] I then pointed out that, sadly, we seem all too capable of putting all sorts of things before God, thereby cluttering up the true vision of ourselves and our relationships with God and with others. It takes real intervention by God (and real willingness on our part) to break through this clutter, such that the lines of communication between God and us become clear.

While it's all very nice to ponder and prose on about keeping those lines cleared, the thing is much easier said than done. This is especially true when the overwhelming evidence before us—from Eden until now—suggests that making strange gods for and of ourselves is something that comes to human beings as naturally and easily as taking a breath, expelling it, and taking another. And the most painful truth is that the first and most difficult idol to dislodge is the idol of oneself. G. K. Chesterton wrote that while we might understand the cosmos, "The self is more distant than any star."[2] God is a mystery, but we, at least, have a few clues about him. He is all love, for one thing, which is why we—who are often messed up in our understanding of love—find him so incomprehensible that we focus back on ourselves, only to be further mystified. We want, but we know not what we want—it's Augustine's restless heart, again—and so we strike out in a kind of blindness, grabbing on to whatever seems like it might tell us who we are, where we belong, and, thereby, create an access to the love we crave. "Hey, God's all very nice, but what about me and what I want and what makes me happy?" It would be an interesting exercise, perhaps, to try to keep count of how many times a day we say (or think) the word *I* or *me*. Our demonstrated narcissism would likely leave us appalled, especially if we put our numbers up against how many times we'd thought of God or anyone else throughout the same day. We are, by far, our favorite and most fascinating subjects.

Speaking of *me* and *I*, allow me to—with a perfect appreciation of the irony—share about myself.

When I first began to pray—and I am forever a beginner—I struggled with focus, particularly in contemplation and in praying the Rosary. I let the struggle take more of my attention than it should have, until praying seemed like a nice idea, but clearly one meant for other people, and not for me, with my head full of monkey chatter and shiny things. When I said as much to an elderly nun named Sister Alice, she smiled and said, "Distraction in prayer is overcome in God's good time, but it is actually one of the easiest things to manage. You must first be willing to admit that you are imperfect. Then, when the distractions come, you simply recognize them for what they are, and bring your attention back to prayer."

I expressed some disbelief. After all, entire tomes have been written about the practice of contemplation, and she was breaking it down to a sentence! Sister was certainly—and understandably—dumbing it down for me, I thought. But she insisted she was not. "To pray is to love," she said, "and that is the easiest and most difficult thing to do. When you are distracted in prayer, imagine a mother gently putting her finger under the chin of a distracted child and simply guiding its attention back where it belongs: no guilt and no remonstrance. You just go on."

The distraction and the correction, she meant, are only the merest moment in a dialogue with eternity—no high drama required.

The Sermon on the Mount reminds me of Sister Alice's instruction; Jesus is teaching us not only to focus but also to actively cast aside the things that stand between God and ourselves. And what are they, really?

Mostly they are ideas, and our ideas are full of *I. Ideas*
are what first pull our attention away from God and
from the wonder of knowing him. And then, because
they are our ideas (or we soon come to believe they
are), we engage with them passionately, forming them
into idols, like golden calves.

Just as we must get rid of our distractions in prayer,
we must dissolve the ideas that have become idols
before we can approach the altar of God. As Jesus says,

> if you bring your gift to the altar, and there
> recall that your brother has anything against
> you, leave your gift there at the altar, go first
> and be reconciled with your brother, and
> then come and offer your gift. (Mt 5:23–24)

We catch Jesus here, mid-instruction. Before he
reaches this point, he has identified for us the nature
of our idols—those things God will not have before
him. Backing up a bit, we read in Matthew:

> You have heard that it was said to your ances-
> tors, "You shall not kill; and whoever kills
> will be liable to judgment." But I say to you,
> whoever is angry with his brother will be
> liable to judgment, and whoever says to his
> brother, "Raqa," will be answerable to the
> Sanhedrin, and whoever says, "You fool,"
> will be liable to fiery Gehenna. (Mt 5:21–22)

And moving ahead we read:

> You have heard that it was said, "You shall
> not commit adultery." But I say to you,
> everyone who looks at a woman with lust
> has already committed adultery with her in
> his heart. If your right eye causes you to sin,

tear it out and throw it away. It is better for
you to lose one of your members than to
have your whole body thrown into Gehenna.
And if your right hand causes you to sin, cut
it off and throw it away. It is better for you to
lose one of your members than to have your
whole body go into Gehenna. (Mt 5:28–30)

This exhortation to cast off body parts is a dramatic
call to put aside the entertainings of our mind when
they have become strange gods—when they have helped
us stumble away from the greatest commandment and
into the sway of our own desires and imaginings, which
necessitate those other "shalt not" commandments.

It is interesting to ponder for a moment both the
order of the Ten Commandments and Jesus' famous
sermon. While it is certainly the case that all the sins
warned against in the Decalogue are serious, there does
seem to be a bit of a hierarchy to them. Murder is a
crime against God and humanity, and it is obviously a
pretty big deal—certainly a bigger deal than coveting
your neighbor's donkey. And yet, this is not the first or
second or even the third commandment. It's not even
the first "You shall not." The warning against strange
gods is the first of those. Both the greatest commandment and the Sermon the Mount do not present things
like murder as root sins. The true roots of sin, the roots
that grow into actions like murder, are seeded within
the mind, which is where idolatry always begins.

No idol is constructed in the *act* of murder. Rather,
the murder is, at its end, an offering to an idol. The
real idol is the enlarged anger within us, and it forms
through our willingness to sustain an idea about our

righteousness and, therefore, an idea about *ourselves*. We cling to resentment or feed jealousy until it grows into something we burnish daily with our justifications. We get it to glitter in our minds like something alive, like a genuine force outside of ourselves. We go so far as to proselytize our grudges to others through spin, gossip, and even lies—see my anger, my resentment, my jealousy, and my spite! Acknowledge it with me; let us have communion in our shared umbrage! Worship me with me! The great evil of murder, then, is the fruit of the idolatry that is first an idea, and the idea is almost always about the self:

- I am angry because I have been disrespected.
- I resent her success while my efforts are ignored.
- He hurt someone I love; I will have vengeance.
- I am afraid of this; I am better than that.
- I, I, I . . .

Even if the murderous thought lasts for but an instant, allowing it—and a thousand ideas like it—can be compared to shaking dandelion fluff. It is visually gratifying to let the wispy seedlings blow about, but eventually weeds take root.

An idea—a thought alone, Jesus warns us—is sufficiently evil to lead us astray, to keep us from loving God with our whole heart and mind and soul. Jesus says that to look on another with lust is the same as committing adultery. How? Because the actual act of commission is the mere end product; it is the sacrifice to the luminous image in our own mind's eye: the image of the pretty girl that craves me; the image of the hunky man being available for me; the image of the ideal object of desire actually wanting me, which makes *me* ideal as well. It makes me perfect and like a god. Objectifying another (whether we do so in lust or in anger) is a key component to idolatry, but that object is most often not the idol. Oftentimes, the strange god placed before the Creator is oneself.

Jesus wants us to get out of our own way. He wants us to take the wayward thoughts that divert our footsteps towards the *I*—the crowded detours that eventually will trap us far from God—and cast them aside. He wants us to deprive them of power. Jesus' greatest followers recognized this. In his *Rule*, Saint Benedict of Nursia tells his monks that when evil thoughts arise, they are to "dash them against Christ immediately."[3] It is a sound and helpful image, and one I have used to great effect. I imagine the crucifix after Christ's death, when all has been won, and I see my own hand crashing the harmful thought against the wood of the cross. With a shatter the thought disappears, and I am released from its hold. My angry or enraged or selfish or irrational thought, having encountered in that moment the constant reality of Christ, is instantly gone.

It all takes place in the mind, yes, but my sin was also forming in the mind, so the thought has been destroyed at the source. This is real-time salvation within the eternal dialogue.

Managing a measure of control over our thoughts and emotions helps us to contain our potential for making new strange gods. As with Sister Alice's instruction on prayer, doing so begins with awareness and a willingness to admit our imperfections. If we practice this consistently, something wonderful happens; instead of making false moves in the shadowy glow of the idol, we become the light of the world.

We know this because Jesus says it. Where we are separated from the glory of God, we are salt that has lost its savor. We are light hidden under a bushel basket, dwindling and then dying from lack of oxygen. Going back to the beginning of chapter five of Matthew's gospel, we find Jesus praising those determined to cast out the idols of self and remain light for the world:

> Blessed are the poor in spirit,
>   for theirs is the kingdom of heaven.
>
> Blessed are they who mourn,
>   for they will be comforted.
>
> Blessed are the meek,
>   for they will inherit the land.
>
> Blessed are they who hunger and thirst for righteousness,
>   for they will be satisfied.
>
> Blessed are the merciful,
>   for they will be shown mercy.
>
> Blessed are the clean of heart
>   for they will see God.
>
> Blessed are the peacemakers,
>   for they will be called children of God.
>
> Blessed are you when they insult you and persecute you and utter every kind of evil against you (falsely) because of me. Rejoice and be glad, for your reward will be great in heaven. Thus they persecuted the prophets who were before you. (Mt 5:3–12)

I confess that all of my life I have suffered through the beatitudes, whether reading them or hearing them read or—God help me that I am so uncharitable—enduring them sung with piano accompaniment. To me these verses have always seemed like a nice preamble to a bigger, greater revelation. They seemed to break down to something an old uncle might growl to us children while in his cups of a winter's night, "Yer all great; God love ya."

My perception, of course, was due to a lack of thinking, prayer, and study. Because of those omissions, I developed a slight irreverence for Christ's words. Peering down the list of beatitudes, I would think, "But that's all of us! We're all of those things!" And then, because my brain runs to the shiny and superficial, the synapses would fire, and I would hear that each one of us is "a brain, an athlete, a basket case, a princess, and a criminal. Sincerely yours, the Breakfast Club."[4] Soon I was singing to myself the old song "Don't You Forget About Me." Sometimes during a homily, I might jerk myself back into the mass with a tsk and a "sorry, Lord . . . I did forget about you," gratefully remembering Sister Alice and the finger under the chin.

It is true that the beatitudes are "all of us" at some point or another. We really are all peacemakers or mourners or show-ers of mercy in our turn; but I was wrong to think them unrelated to the rest of the Sermon on the Mount. The beatitudes are the promise of what is ours, in all of those aspects of ourselves, once we have cast off the attachments to ideas, the idols Jesus illustrates throughout the Sermon, that keep us so self-involved and forever fragmented. If we are attentive to

Christ's call for detachment—not so much from our limbs and eyes but from our furies and fancies—we remain more closely aligned with God, more direct in our focus, and more mindful of keeping God alone before us. There we find our potential for wholeness and more. The detachment means we are less inclined to covetousness, and thus we are poor in spirit, and we gain the kingdom.

The surrender of our passions gentles us, which attracts us to what is good, rather than what should repel.

Our mourning becomes less self-indulgent and informed by a consoling hope.

Our thirst for righteousness is emptied of our own self-indulgent wrath, which we entrust to God's judgment, so that the work of quenching that thirst may be pure.

Our mercy means we are not clinging to murderous ideas, and by letting go of them, we create room for God's own mercy in us.

Our purity of heart means we look upon God, undistracted, and thus we see him.

As peacemakers, we renounce our interests in the spoils of victory and take no pleasure in anyone's defeat—like Christ himself.

And if we are persecuted for all of this, it will be a validation that we are no longer belonging to the world but are fully God's own.

This finally explains the paradoxical coda with which Jesus ties up his list: be happy to be abused, persecuted, and lied about because you are no longer ensnared and enslaved by the idols of your mind or the ideas of anyone else. You have been freed from the shackles of conformity; you've come detached from the ever-whirling collective. Rejoice, then, and be glad; your ideas have been dashed against Christ, and you have escaped the snare of the idols. And if you are not being abused, persecuted, and lied about, you can take it as evidence that, as a kitty might say on the Internet, "You're doing it wrong."

Well, we mostly are doing it wrong. That almost can't be helped, largely because we do not realize all the ways in which we've become ensnared and enslaved or just how many of our ideas need to come into hard contact with that shattering cross.

CHAPTER**THREE**

The Idol of the Idea

A friend once asked me how I would define myself, and I said, "Short, fat, and graying."

"Not *describe*," she corrected. "Define. How do you define yourself?"

That was more difficult. Over the course of my life I have defined myself—sometimes with regrettable pride and narrow-minded passion—as a New Yorker, an Irish woman, a liberal, a feminist, a Democrat, a Catholic, a mother, a student, a healer, a Yankee fan, a manager, a Christian, a post-feminist—the list goes on and on. Wanting to continually grow and change, we can easily get caught up in how we define ourselves, but hopefully we never remain static.

One thing that can hinder growth is our willingness to attach labels to ourselves and adopt identifications, particularly with groups, to whose ideas we've become attached. In doing so, we cease to ponder, cease to wonder, cease to think. Remember Saint Gregory of Nyssa: only wonder leads to truly knowing. When we over-identify with an idea or hermetically seal ourselves within the seemingly safe cocoon of groupthink, we stop knowing much at all. Everything we think we know is surrendered to the collective from which we gladly take our identities and our self-definitions. Like the *Star Trek* villains, the Borg, we assimilate into our lives the ideas, manners, and views of the set. Resistance is futile. The collective becomes a prismatic idol that colors and distorts our view of everything, including the way to God and the very people before us, in whom we are meant to see and serve God.

About twenty years ago, my husband and I were involved with the creation of a new Catholic parish. On the pastoral team was a very warm, friendly, and hard-working Sister, who in the beginning acted not only as the director of religious education, but also as chief liturgist and, for a time, honorary lead guitar player. It is difficult to take issue with someone who is working tirelessly and with great dedication toward the building of community; but, some members of the parish did manage to feel unpersuaded by—and a bit uncomfort-able with—a few of Sister's ideas, most glaringly with her insistence that the liturgy contain as few gender references as possible. This approach to the liturgy led to a Gloria that some (including me) found grating on the ear. "Glory to God in the highest, and peace to God's people on earth" tripped up the congregation for years, and many took the changes to be obstinate point-making.

Because I respected her greatly and was, in truth, a little intimidated by her self-assurance, I had to work up the nerve to broach the subject with her while we

painted an office together. "I get what you're doing,"
I said, "but don't you think it's a bit of overkill on the
Gloria? I mean, we sing, 'Lord Jesus Christ, only Son
of the Father . . . seated at the right hand of the Father.'
If God is Father, is it so awful to sing, 'And peace to
his people on earth' as well? It's just being consistent."

She gave a respectful answer that covered feminine
sensibilities and dysfunctional family relationships, all
of which made male pronouns problematic and seemingly insensitive for some. I had my own long-standing
feminist leanings, and they allowed me to accept her
explanation—but not wholly and not comfortably.

A few months later, during a parish dinner to thank
all the volunteers, I found myself sitting next to Sister,
and, a little better (or worse) for wine, I approached the
subject again, declaring that the inconsistencies—particularly within the setting of a liturgical prayer—were
still nagging at me.

"You don't understand," Sister answered kindly.
"There are a lot of people who have terrible, hurtful
relationships with their fathers, and over-identifying
God with maleness creates a block; it gets in the way
of the relationship they seek with God."

"But Sister," I said, "where does that leave someone
like me, someone who has had a terrible, hurtful relationship with an earthly father, and so is very grateful to
be consoled by the notion of having a heavenly father
to turn to?"

I can still see the way her expression opened and her
eyes widened as she sat back. "That's a fair point," she
said with sincerity. "That's the first time I have ever
heard anyone say that."

"Well, you need to get out more," I ribbed her, "and broaden your circle of friends."

It was a joke, obviously. Sister lived in community with other members of her order, and it is understandable that similarly aged women would be like-minded in their thinking, but this community had embraced their idea so wholeheartedly they'd stopped wondering whether there might be other perspectives out there. Because they'd stopped wondering, they couldn't know that, as Sister admitted that night, another perspective could have validity. And that meant there was a whole swath of people within the Body of Christ—people they were eager and willing to serve for the sake of Christ— whom they simply had not seen because of the idol that had arisen from her community's idea.

I would like to say my argument made a difference to the Gloria, but it didn't. There was another moment, though, when Sister considered that perhaps her notions needed adjusting after all. When the pastor asked her to pick the tiles for the restrooms, she chose a lovely gray-and-blue combination for the men's room and a terrifyingly bilious yellow-and-brown combination for the ladies. At their unveiling, one woman after another stumbled out of the bathroom worriedly asking, "Look at me! Do I look sick? Am I dying?" The awful color and the fluorescent lights cast a jaundiced pall over everyone, and we soon learned to avert our eyes while washing our hands, and to do without freshening our lipstick. Sister was mortified and terribly apologetic. "I never imagined it would look so bad," she groaned. "I was just trying to get away from the pink and the rose—it was so stereotypically feminine!"

"That's not a bad thing," we told her. "Pink makes us look healthy, not nauseous!"

"I know, I know."

We loved Sister, but when she was eventually reassigned, it seemed unfair that we could not somehow send her off with that stomach-spinning bathroom—the product of an idol grown too large to live in the light.

We all do what Sister did, to varying extremes. We cling to ideas long past the point of what is healthy or reasonable, and we set them before us, daring anyone to knock them down. I once heard a new pastor complain about a dreaded first meeting with his pastoral team and liturgy committee. "In every parish," he sighed, "the first thing they want a priest to do is bow down to the god of 'but we've always done it this way.'"

When we over-identify with our thoughts, the result is always inhibition, narrowness, and constraint, instead of the freedom that resides in a trusting and true relationship with God. Such over-identification always leads to a cramped "no" rather than a joyful "yes," even if the idea initially seems broad-minded and permissive.

That even our best attempts at reform and change can become narrow and oppressive seems counterintuitive. People have become so accustomed to the idea of faith—and particularly organized religion—as a thing that shackles and says only "no," they can't wrap their minds around the fact that everything about God is positive, from alpha to omega and back. But the evidence of the positive coming from God resides in the very fact of creation, which grew on the yes of God's own intention.

The world came to be because God consented to it being. Our Lord, and the whole beautiful pageant of our salvation, came to be because Mary consented to it. Isn't it interesting to ponder that God is not pushy. He sought the consent of his own creatures in order to incarnate and dwell among them. God seeks out our yes because it is most like him; it creates more unto abundance. Within our faith communities—particularly if we are open to hearing the wisdom of those who have come before us, rather than insisting on our own notions—we come to understand this more fully. We discover that if commandments and teachings seem heavy on the "shall nots," those words are not actually about God or Church saying no. Rather, they are warnings about what takes us away from God, what creates distance—the actions (born of ideas) that say no to him, no to others, and yes only to ourselves, which makes our world very small indeed.

To say yes to God is to say yes to the very essence of what is positive, expansive, and cocreative—and for anything creative to happen, there must first be space. A wonderful Anglican hymn begins, "There is a wideness in God's mercy." Both wideness and mercy are formed within yes.

What has "no" ever created, besides hell? And what is hell founded upon but the no born of a prideful idea of self that became an idol and drew beings, willfully, away from God. Having been offered the breadth and depth of vast creation; having lived with and for truth that is bright, alive, and sometimes scary in its ever-newness, angelic beings settled for the stultifying sameness of self, and then we humans did it, too. We settled for ideas that do not grow and opportunities that do not appear. We settled for atrophied potentialities, which, perhaps, seemed safer to hoard to the self rather than offer to God, who with our every consent expands creation.

Nothing grows in no. A family member, a very bright and gifted girl, went through a fairly usual period, beginning in middle school. She had bought into the idea that it was not cool to study or get good grades. She put away the books, brought out the eyeliner, and essentially said no to all of her gifts. Why? In order to fit in with the weak-but-typically-cool idea that—informed by cynicism—she already knew all she needed to know, and anyone who did not know it was not cool. But there were so many rules to being cool and cynical. It was not the freeing experience she had imagined it to be. There was a constant call for conformity, a continual demand to disdain, and a lessening of human feeling. She was not at liberty to betray simple excitement and enthusiasm, which, though human and true, were not considered to be cool emotions.

Eventually when she had begun college and discovered she needed remedial classes before she could even begin studying for her degree, she stopped saying no to what came naturally to her. She said yes to her gifts and lived in their truth—which is where God lives, because he is all truth—even though she was unsure where it all would lead. It led to freedom, but first she had to cast aside an idol born of what had seemed, at the time, such a great idea.

The things we perceive as "no" coming from God or religion are simply serious advisements meant to free us from the power of our own propensities to navel-gaze and fixate on our ideas and desires, so that we will be able to receive all God wants to give us.

> For I know well the plans I have in mind for you . . . plans for your welfare, not for woe! plans to give you a future full of hope. When you call me, when you go to pray to me, I will listen to you. When you look for me, you will find me. Yes, when you seek me with all your heart, you will find me . . . and I will change your lot. (Jer 29:11–14)

Pope Benedict XVI has written,

> We can understand properly what the kingship of Jesus Christ means only if we trace its origin in the Old Testament, where we immediately discover a surprising fact. It is obvious that God did not intend Israel to have a kingdom. The kingdom was, in fact, a result of Israel's rebellion against God and against his prophets, a defection from the original will of God. The law was to be Israel's king, and through the law, God himself. . . . But Israel was jealous of the neighboring peoples with their powerful kings. . . . Surprisingly, God yielded to Israel's obstinacy and so devised a new kind of kingship for them. The son of David, the king, is Jesus: in him God entered humanity and espoused it to himself.[1]

We get ideas, and we embrace them and pet them and polish them until they own us and hinder us, and we are no longer free. God—far from punishing us for having ideas—works to reach past the strange gods, to keep us with him. He says yes to the idea of a king, and delivers himself, incarnate of a virgin who said yes (and who, in doing so, taught us the great lesson that our yes to God is always answered with his own yes). And then this king says yes to a torturous consummation of love that weds his Church to him forever.

But why? Why does he do this? Only for love. We humans can't help ourselves. We naturally try to make sense of our world by putting everything, including God, love, and life, into manageable compartments. Then we label these compartments and hide within our ideas, which we have come to worship, because those, at least, we think we understand.

But God—who created a world of order that far surpasses our attempts at order—points his cannons at those heaping compartments and goes "ba-boom!" And when we ask (because we never learn), "Why did you do that when I had it all so beautifully planned, thought out, and settled?" God says, "It was blocking my love. My love couldn't reach you with all that stuff in the way."

CHAPTER**FOUR**

The Idol of Prosperity

> Do not store up for yourselves treasures on
> earth, where moth and decay destroy, and
> thieves break in and steal. But store up
> treasures in heaven, where neither moth
> nor decay destroys, nor thieves break in
> and steal. For where your treasure is, there
> also will your heart be.

MATTHEW 6:19–21

Once, while attending a Catholic media conference, I passed by the booth of a favorite publisher and saw the vendor was giving away small, detachable book jackets meant to cover a wonderful monthly devotional magazine. I slipped one into my swag bag—the jacket had a black cover with an embossed image of Jesus on it—and didn't think of it again until I got home and removed the cellophane wrapping to discover that the thing was actually made of a good-quality leather (it smelled wonderful) and contained not one but two sturdy gold ribbons with which to mark pages. I was so ridiculously pleased with it that I went on Facebook and extolled the cover's praises. I wrote that "if we are living in a material world, then I am a material girl; this cover makes me so happy!"

People who really know me laughed because I am someone who owns two pairs of shoes—both of which are plastic Crocs—and a pair of flip-flops. My son once shook his head and said, "Please tell me you did not wear Crocs when you spoke at the Vatican." To which I replied, "What? They're comfy. They look like Mary Janes. Besides, if anyone was looking at my feet while I was speaking, it means I made a poor job of my talk, and, therefore, I have much more important things to worry about."

So I don't own leather shoes or, for that matter, a leather handbag. But for my monthly devotional magazine, I have a leather cover, and even now that it is well broken in, I still occasionally take a sniff of the leather. For reasons beyond my ken, I still take a most unseemly delight in it, and that reality has made me wonder if I am, in fact, a much more materialistic person than I or anyone else might have suspected. Am I just as inclined as the most conspicuous consumer to put too much store in mere things? Perhaps my lack of possessions reflect not a true discipline of poverty, but mere eccentricities in my tastes.

The same, I think, might be true for my husband. On the surface, we both seem pretty detached. I drive the "new car," which is more than ten years old; my husband's car is from the last century. I have my Crocs. He has only essential footwear. Both of us wear our clothes for as many years as they last and never think to shop for more until we really must. We work this way with regard to most of the stuff in our lives. We limit the house to one television and then keep the thing until it dies.

But for all that, if we begin to delude ourselves that we are nonmaterialistic paragons, we need only recall that we suffer from an excess of sentimentalism and still have books of matches, perfectly untouched, from weddings we attended in 1984. The hammock I bought my husband five years ago still looks like new because he never uses it. He hauls it out the beginning of summer and then brings it in when it looks like rain. Then he brings it out again. And then in, again. He quickly tires of that routine, so by mid-July the thing stays in for good. I keep telling him that he can leave the hammock out to get rained on, and that it's not meant to last forever; but his heart would break to see it become weathered, unpretty, and old. Perhaps he doesn't want it to seem aged because evidence of something aging means we are aging too. If we can keep a thing looking new forever, we can indulge in an illusion that we, too, will last forever.

Forever comes with a catch though: my husband is so busy saving the hammock that its usefulness is lost to him. It's like he doesn't have a hammock at all. Forever, then, is a very empty idol.

In the Gospel of Matthew 16:25, Jesus said, "Whoever wishes to save his life will lose it." He was warning us that holding on to anything too tightly—our lives and the stuff in it—will prevent us from being able to open ourselves up to him. A willingness to let it all go,

on the other hand, leaves us with room for him and for
the fullness he promises. We can't reach out to the real
God while hugging the fake ones to our chests.

As a Benedictine oblate, I try to live with a sort of
"monastic mindfulness" as much as I can within my
station. I'm not very good at it, truth be told (It com-
forts me to know that intention does count.), but I do
try to remember what Saint Benedict of Nursia wrote
in his *Rule* and adapt it to my life. In chapter 33, he
wrote on "Whether Monks Ought to Have Anything
of Their Own":

> This vice [of personal ownership] especially
> is to be cut out of the monastery by the
> roots. Let no one presume to give or receive
> anything without the Abbot's leave, or to
> have anything as his own . . . but for all their
> necessities let them look to the Father of the
> monastery. And let it be unlawful to have
> anything which the Abbot has not given or
> allowed. Let all things be common to all, as it
> is written, and let no one say or assume that
> anything is his own.[1]

For those of us who are not monastic, that may
sound extreme; but remember that monasticism is a
voluntary giving up of things and possessions, coupled
with a surrender of one's own will, for building up a
community and developing a humble acquiescence to
God's will in all things. As an oblate living in the world,
I am mindful of Benedict's words urging me to resist
cluttering up my life with anything that seems superflu-
ous to my actual needs. This is a good mindset for any
Christian to take on, particularly in a world of big-box

stores and nonstop media invitations to "buy this, buy more, buy bigger, buy two, buy it more often, and buy it today!" Because Saint Benedict was a sensible man, he wrote a sensible *Rule*. In it, he acknowledged that while attachments and ownership are to be minimized as much as possible, some monks will simply have more need of material things than others. But, Benedict said, instead of this being a source of pride, it should be a source of humility, because it is better to need less. Every worldly, earthly thing you "need" is something else that can come between you and God. "Whoever needs less should thank God and not be distressed, but whoever needs more should feel humble because of his weakness, not self-important because of the kindness shown him. In this way all the members will be at peace."[2]

So, for example, a monk who can't quite handle the Lenten fast and is permitted more food should not think of himself as advantaged for his singularity, because all the extra food really emphasizes is his greater need. Conversely, the monk who can handle the fast should not begrudge the first monk his extras, since the extras are not a sign of privilege. Or, a monk who finds he cannot go to sleep without a nightlight is not at an advantage because he gets a light, but neither should he be judged negatively; he is only more needful than the monk who has no fear of the dark.

This can be a difficult way to view the world. It is an almost upside-down way of thinking, but perhaps where material things and notions of "wealth" and "the good life" are concerned, the world needs to be stood on its head a little. This is particularly true in America where the promise of financial and material reward has long allured impoverished people and invited them to dream large. Our own ambitions, coupled with a Calvinistic work ethic that has defined the nation since its founding, has created the driven-to-succeed culture where success is too often measured by the trappings of material excess. We strive to purchase all the things we are told we need if we are to be happy.

Trappings indeed! This mindset has become a kind of prison for people in every economic sphere. The very wealthy "haves" become defensive when discussion arises about their excess. They resort to pointing out that they (or their forebears) "earned" all their stuff. Then they cling to what they own, as though possessions mean anything, or can protect them, or can give evidence of their superior worth. Meanwhile, the "have-nots" are encouraged to resent all that excess and privilege, and yet they still desire it for themselves. From a distance of almost 1,500 years, Saint Benedict tells us the people who have so much are to be pitied because excess is evidence of their need.

Blessed Teresa of Calcutta put a more modern spin on how possessions can entrap. Although she spent decades in service to the poorest of the poor, she noted that the poor are capable of finding contentment in their lives in ways the wealthy cannot. The poor can do this because the action of love in their lives is not fighting to be known and recognized amid a blockade of love substitutes.

> The spiritual poverty of the Western World is much greater than the physical poverty of our people. . . . You, in the West, have

millions of people who suffer such terrible loneliness and emptiness. They feel unloved and unwanted.

These people are not hungry in the physical sense, but they are in another way. They know they need something more than money, yet they don't know what it is. What they are missing, really, is a living relationship with God.[3]

A family member of mine—a fellow with a good education and a career that compensated him well—was nevertheless in a constant state of debt. His credit cards were always charged to the max because he was forever buying new stuff to replace the stuff he already had—stuff that had quickly bored him. He spirit was restless, and I always suspected that the restlessness was rooted in that mindset of earthly success that could do wonders for filling an empty room but not much for filling an empty heart. The life of faith, which attracted him on some level—if his Sunday was free, he would go to church—did not appeal to his social set. In any case, it was routinely overshadowed, if not obliterated, by what was worldly, glamorous, and, in the end, quite temporary. When he died and the family was tasked with clearing out his belongings, the job was a monumental undertaking. Walking from attic to basement, from cluttered room to cluttered room, we kept asking each other, "How can one man have so much stuff? Why did he need all of this?"

The answer, I thought then and still think now, was that there was a void in his life he could not fill on his own, no matter how much material stuff he threw into it. Although he had many friends and was dearly loved by the whole family, there was an emptiness that had gone unanswered. He was a victim of the exact spiritual poverty Blessed Teresa described. He was a privileged member of the community whose extras, as Saint Benedict taught, were only evidence of the depths of his need and his entrapment by all he possessed. It reminded me a bit of the famous quote by Dostoyevsky in *The Brothers Karamazov:*

> The world says: "You have needs, therefore satisfy them, for you have the same rights as the richest and noblest men. Do not be afraid to satisfy them, but even increase them"— this is the current teaching of the world. And in this they see freedom. But what comes of this right to increase one's need? For the rich, isolation and spiritual suicide; for the poor, envy and murder. . . .[4]

It is simplicity that brings real freedom. As a Benedictine nun at Abbaye Notre Dame l'Annonciation put it, "I really loved clothes! But there's freedom in wearing my habit."[5] There is freedom in what is simple; having less leaves room for something so much greater.

The world tells us to want more and more, and praises us when we acquire it. It holds us up as winners of life's lottery and of the American Dream. But when the possessions get in the way of our ability to develop a living relationship with God, we have lost a great deal to these empty, pretty idols of prosperity, which we have allowed to stand before him.

Prosperity is not evil in and of itself. A wealthy nation is one that can respond quickly and effectively to help another nation in crisis. A wealthy philanthropist can do a great deal of good for others. It was the wealthy Joseph of Arimathea who had the coin, the connections, and the clout to have Jesus' tortured body removed from the cross, shrouded in fine linen, and entombed before the Sabbath. All of this was essential to the Resurrection. But prosperity can be a fast and powerful vehicle for driving us away from what Christ has told us is essential—which does not include getting rich.

> Then he told them a parable. "There was a rich man whose land produced a bountiful harvest. He asked himself, 'What shall I do, for I do not have space to store my harvest?' And he said, 'This is what I shall do: I shall tear down my barns and build larger ones. There I shall store all my grain and other goods and I shall say to myself, "Now as for you, you have so many good things stored up for many years, rest, eat, drink, be merry!"' But God said to him, 'You fool, this night your life will be demanded of you; and the things you have prepared, to whom will they belong?' Thus will it be for the one who stores up treasure for himself but is not rich in what matters to God." (Lk 12:16–21)

When we are wealthy, we are segregated from ordinary people and ordinary realities, things like standing in lines, struggling with bills, and relying on mass transit. We stop identifying with those from whom we are separated. When we can no longer identify with others, we can begin to dehumanize them. When we dehumanize others, we lose sight of God, for we are made in his image, and thus we embrace a dreadful spiritual poverty in which we see only ourselves as a divine image. Rather than our world becoming enlarged, it becomes smaller. Our circle of acquaintances becomes more select, which means our perspective becomes diminished as well. Surrounded by others who are accustomed to hearing only yes and who believe they are charting their own destinies (absent any bothersome God), we turn away from our better angels. And then we become lonely, and we do not know why.

Perhaps one of the most frightening things about America and, I suppose, much of the West, is the message we send to the world: if only everyone could be raised to a particular standard of wealth, happiness would be the inevitable result. Prosperity equals pleasure, and cash equals contentment. But there is scant evidence this is true. On any given day, we can pull up a gossip site and read about fabulously wealthy, privileged people who are miserably unhappy. We read about formerly brilliant artists whose lives have become so celebrated and self-indulgent that they no longer have anything pertinent to say. Even if they did, they wouldn't dream of departing from the scripts of their social set because as far as human beings are concerned, their peers are all they have. The big loneliness lurks just behind them.

When my husband and I were newly wed, and he was beginning his engineering career, I bought him a poster for his office. It was a picture of a frog climbing upward, and the caption read, "Somewhere in the world, there's a pedestal with my name on it." It was silly and cheesy, and we have made a running joke of it for decades, particularly once the raises and promotions began to come his way. "Here comes the pedestal!" we would say. For a while, he dreamed of making it into the upper echelons of management—the place where decisions are made, riches and privileges are enjoyed and—best of all—power is wielded. He put a great deal of focus and energy into this goal until the trajectory of his career had power over him—enough to sway him toward pride when things were going well or plunge him into doubt and anger when they were not. But then something funny happened. Every time he got close to the powerful, rather than be attracted, he found himself repelled. Their valuations seemed incompatible with his, and eventually he realized that if the goal could be achieved, it might well prove empty. Even worse, it would take him from the family activities and the volunteer work he loved, without satisfying him half as much. Having never read the *Rule of Saint Benedict*, he instinctively understood that less was more and that the sort of power he prefers in his life is the one connected to something beyond this world.

Dorothy Day, cofounder of the Catholic Worker Movement, was also a Benedictine oblate. A better oblate than I, she managed over the course of her life to divest herself of ownership to a remarkable degree. She lived in extremely humble housing and dressed herself in donated clothes. When she traveled, she was known for bringing only two things with her—her breviary for praying the Liturgy of the Hours, and a jar of instant coffee. (Talk about self-abnegation!) Divesting herself of material things, she also rejected prestige, power, and offices. (Given her influence, her connections, and the

high regard many held for her intelligence and energy,
she could have had them.) She encouraged others to
reject power and its trappings, too, because she knew
them for the false gods of busy-bodiness and tyranny
they were.

The Orthodox Christian writer Jim Forest tells a
great story in an essay titled, "What I Learned about
Justice from Dorothy Day":

> Tom Cornell tells the story of a donor com-
> ing into the Catholic Worker and giving
> Dorothy a diamond ring. Dorothy thanked
> her for it and put it in her pocket. Later a
> rather demented lady came in, one of the
> more irritating regulars at the house. Doro-
> thy took the diamond ring out of her pocket
> and gave it to the woman. Someone on the
> staff said to Dorothy, "Wouldn't it have been
> better if we took the ring to the diamond
> exchange, sold it, and paid that woman's rent
> for a year?" Dorothy replied that the woman
> had her dignity and could do what she liked
> with the ring. She could sell it for rent money
> or take a trip to the Bahamas. Or she could
> enjoy wearing a diamond ring on her hand
> like the woman who gave it away. "Do you
> suppose," Dorothy asked, "that God created
> diamonds only for the rich?"[6]

Did I mention that Day was a Benedictine oblate?
Whenever I remember that story, I imagine Benedict
of Nursia up in heaven, smiling in approval and saying,
"Oh, *snap*, Dorothy. There's my girl!"

Day was much too grounded to entertain idols; she
didn't make them of the intellectuals whom she inspired

or the poor whom she served. As Forest relates, she kept her worship for God:

> When I think of her, I think of her first of all on her knees praying before the Blessed Sacrament. I think of those long lists of names she kept of people, living and dead, to pray for. I think of her at Mass, I think of her praying the rosary, I think of her going off for Confession each Saturday evening.
>
> "We feed the hungry, yes," she said. "We try to shelter the homeless and give them clothes, but there is strong faith at work; we pray. If an outsider who comes to visit us doesn't pay attention to our prayings and what that means, then he'll miss the whole point."[7]

The whole point is this: when we have cleared away the idols we have placed before God—imagine using your arm and just sweeping away all those trophies from the mantle so that there is nothing between us and him—we open up a direct line to the God who is all in all. He is all love, all mercy, all light, all power, all compassion, all goodness, and all wealth. God is the God of all our longings fulfilled, in whom no voids remain. And that is all God wants and needs from us—our willingness to keep the direct line open so that he may be with us and be all of those things for us, with nothing standing between our love.

Those who pray the Liturgy of the Hours are always startled when they encounter the First Antiphon in the Office of Readings, for Tuesday of Week II, which reads, "Surrender to God, and he will do everything for you." To clear away the idols is to give God access to us and to our needs, and to trust him with them. It is just that simple; there is no ulterior motive. He wants nothing for us but our good.

CHAPTER**FIVE**

The Idol of Technology

There is an amusing cartoon that pops up all over the Internet, particularly on Facebook. Someone is saying that "it's two o'clock in the morning; come to bed!" In the picture, a stick figure is staring at a computer monitor, tapping away at the keyboard. "I can't," the figure says. "Someone on the Internet is wrong!"

It is a terrific summation of certain kinds of idolatry—both of ideas and technology. It shows us that the Internet, particularly social media, serves our idolatry by assisting in our fascinated pseudo-engagement with others. Or more precisely, the Internet assists our obsessed engagement with ourselves by disguising it as a fascination with others who—either by offering opposition or validation—keep us fixated on the self. All those social media friends who confirm our every thought, all those tweeting followers who make it seem like our ideas matter in the grand scheme of things, are like so many shiny trophies and mirrors, reflecting back at us what we think of as our best and truest selves.

The Internet is a tool of staggering power, and it's a great gift for the gleaning of information and ease of communication; but the Internet might well be the greatest tempter to ego gratification since the hissing serpent of Eden. As such, the Internet is a most cunning inducement to idolatry. Like any good trap, it seems so very passive. We discover it with delight; we engage, we become adept (in some cases, addicted), and are perpetually distracted. The evil one loves distraction—aims for distraction—because it is the means by which we lose track of God and dwell among the idols.

> Now the serpent was the most cunning of all the animals that the LORD God had made. The serpent asked the woman, "Did God really tell you not to eat from any of the trees in the garden?" The woman answered the serpent: "We may eat of the fruit of the trees in the garden; it is only about the fruit of the tree in the middle of the garden that God said, 'You shall not eat it or even touch it, lest you die.'" But the serpent said to the woman: "You certainly will not die! No, God knows well that the moment you eat of it your eyes will be opened and you will be like gods who know what is good and what is bad." (Gn 3:1–5)

On the Internet, we are in many ways like gods. Using the Internet makes us identifiers of what is good! We are able to banish what is evil from our sight by banishing it from our site with the click of a button. We are millions of mini-deities floating through the fiber optics, touching down to speak on the mountaintops of our social media shrines and our combox churches. We feel great while we are there, particularly when our tweet is noticed and passed around with approval, or our drop by is liked and shared. We are so comfortable—so safely cocooned in our established routes, moving from agreeable echo chamber to agreeable echo chamber. We are "followed," "liked," and "pinned" on virtual boards—we feel uncommonly alert, connected in ways we simply are not throughout the rest of our day. Our synapses are firing, our thoughts are lit up, and we flit from venue to venue all day long—with regular stops to check our e-mail—eager to glean the next new thought, the next idea that will keep us diverted from the tiresome, humdrum stuff that makes up the underappreciated gift of everyday life. When we are online, some of us feel more alive than at any other time of the day. That is an insidious illusion, beloved of Satan, who wants us to be delighted, engaged, addicted, and distracted. How can we be alive to God and to the workings of the Holy Spirit, if we are spending hour after hour alive to only ourselves, reveling as our ideas, opinions, and words are reflected back at us, forever and ever, Amen?

This is a problem for those of us who earn our living on the Internet, where taking a break from work often means opening another screen and popping in to one of those social-media outlets. A few decades ago, a coffee break offered a jolt of caffeine and some companionship to boost our sagging energies and raise our productivity. Now, a quick turn at Twitter does much the same thing. Our tired brains get a dose of headlines, a quick shot of opinion, and a few sassy comments from our cyber companions. That gets the mental energies sparking again; we return to our work barking, "Let there be light."

All this engagement is exhausting, and, deep down, we know it is no good for us. Yet we cannot break away, or are unwilling to break away.

I have a friend whose work involves being online for a major portion of the day. She knows that the last place she should allow herself a daily visit is Facebook. Facebook is no good for her. It renders her unproductive. It usually makes her angry. She is aware the site is a place of illusion, misdirection, and, sometimes, malicious distortion. She knows it often brings out the worst in her, separating her from her best intentions to love God and others. Every few months she tries to wean herself from it. "I tell myself I will only go on Facebook in the morning to get news and at night, just to see what the world has been up to," she says. "Even if I manage to do that for a few days, eventually I'm back. The page is always opened and refreshed whenever I have a spare minute—and I am just sucked into it."

I asked her if she realizes that in saying, "See what the world has been up to" she means that the big world—the fascinating world—was the one coming to her through a 19-inch monitor, which was able to draw her attention more completely than a human being standing right before her. She admitted it. "It shames me," she said. "Sometimes I'm listening to someone talking to me in the office, but I'm thinking, 'Just finish talking so I can get back to my stuff.' Of course I'm not thinking of the work stuff but the me stuff, which I can't get enough of."

She pushes away the real world and escapes to the illusions. She rejects what is sometimes dreary, like other people, to delight herself and bathe in the regard of the better, less-troublesome, handpicked others of the Net.

I certainly could not judge my friend because, as someone who makes her living online, I am all too familiar with her plight; it is mine too. Often when writing this book, I have had to resort to a spiral notebook and longhand. It was the only way I could wrest myself from the clutches of the Internet—and all of its noise and distraction and heady validation, which I sometimes call the "Lizzie dizzying praise." I had to tune out in order to ponder the vagaries of idolatry.

O, irony! What do you think has inspired this chapter but my own realization that I have put the very strange god of Internet infotainment before God Almighty— and too often before my God-given family or commitments? I have succumbed to the distracting, destructive power of seeing my own ideas and words erected somewhere, all spruced up and reflecting me back at myself.

Sometimes the Internet reminds me of a house of mirrors I once visited—a maze of me. I turned around and walked into myself. I passed a mirror and jumped at my own reflection. I apologized for intruding only to see I was apologizing to me.

One of the reasons I keep my combox open on my blog (and am loath to unfriend anyone) is that if I didn't have someone telling me a few times a week that I am wrongheaded, obnoxious, dimwitted, narcissistic, or—as someone once said— "a lot more underwhelming than you think you are," I might never get properly grounded. It may be humiliating to open an e-mail and read, "You're not just fat, but stupid, too, and also uncharitable," but it's a necessary humiliation. It forces me to slow down, re-read something I've written, and ask myself, "Was I being uncharitable there? Was that hateful? Am I a preening know-it-all, here?" Sometimes the answer is no and sometimes it's yes, but I think I am better off for the asking and for the inventory. Increasingly, as I look back on my archives, it seems to me I should shut up more.

Of course I think that only when I am not online, when I am not reading, typing, clicking, reading, and typing some more. Once I am online, humility and self-doubt largely disappear, and all those gleaming ideas—out there, in the world—draw me like a raven to a sparkly thing. I am as puny a godling as was ever raised, but my, those sites and shrines do shine!

My friend's words about "the world" (perhaps because I so identified with them), reminded me of something the Trappist monk Thomas Merton wrote: "As long as I assume that the world is something I discover by turning on the radio . . . I am deceived from the start."[1]

Many people take that quotation out of context and use it to slam the wiles and distractions of media, and it certainly does suit the purpose; but Merton was talking about something else entirely. He was talking about the romance of the *idea* of otherness and its sterility. Still, even taking his remarks in context, we can apply them to our discussion here:

> I am, in other words, a man in the modern world. In fact, I am the world just as you are! Where am I going to look for the world first of all if not in myself?
>
> As long as I assume that the world is something I discover by turning on the radio or looking out the window, I am deceived from the start. As long as I imagine that the world is something to be "escaped" in a monastery—that wearing a special costume and following a quaint observance takes me out of this world—I am dedicating my life to an illusion.

We might say something similar about people of faith living with and working on the Internet. Paradoxically, the Internet takes us out of ourselves (and thus our world from where we itch to escape) to place us in the world (which becomes the escape from which we must escape). Merton could just as easily have written:

> As long as I imagine that the world is something to be "escaped" through the Internet—that going by a special handle, blogging, and following quaint new etiquette takes me "into a new, better world," I am dedicating my time to what is false.

The material trappings we think can take us out of the world or into a better one, according to Merton, are always illusory because the world is not out there. Nor can we remove ourselves from this world for a new one. The world is not where our gaze takes us at a window. It is certainly not the glittering things reflecting us back at ourselves. We cannot reasonably expect to find the

world (or something "better than this one" brought
to us through our media paraphernalia) because Christ
Jesus has told us that the kingdom of God—hence,
the entire creation—resides within us, inasmuch as the
Holy Spirit does. The kingdom of God is not outside
of us. We are not outside of it, except as we wish to be;
and thus we allow ourselves to be lured away by one
chimera after another.

Perhaps Saint Augustine said it best when he wrote,
"I found thee not, O Lord, without, because I erred in
seeking thee without that wert within."

Those few words may sum up the whole mystery
of our need to create daily idols. We are from God,
created in his image, loved into being and freedom
and—because that is true—free to look away, to look
"out there" into the world. But if we are alive to God,
we want to bring God with us into the world. We want
to see the world as God sees it and to serve it as God
has self-emptyingly served it—through Christ. It is an
incarnational process that we consent to, mindfully and
with intention. Absent that mindfulness, absent that
intention, we are like amnesiacs stumbling into Times
Square at night: we look out at the world and we have
no point of reference beyond ourselves. Very quickly,
we then seek out anything that pertains to us, places us,
confirms us, or reflects us; the shiny things immediately
bedazzle us, and then we are lost. "Deceived from the
start," as Merton says, we remain lost and deceived
until either we remember who we are, or get some
directions and follow them back to the place of first
knowing, where God and the kingdom reside.

This is the way of every life—this seeking outside of ourselves for placement—because the world is not our natural home. We are, as Saint Elizabeth Ann Seton said, "children of eternity." If God is eternal, then Augustine nailed it, utterly and for all time, when he prayed, "Our heart is restless until it rests in you."

The Internet exploits that restlessness like nothing else yet invented, but the Holy Spirit has a way of using all things—often the most confounding people and tools—for God's intention, which is always to draw us to him and never to push away. If the Net is an instrument of distraction, by which the world and the evil one pull us further away from God and into the idolatry of ideas, it can also be used to guide us back. In fact, in 2010, Pope Benedict XVI so keenly understood the Internet's usefulness to the New Evangelization that he expressly asked Catholics, particularly priests and religious, to jump in and start evangelizing—to, as it were, sign on, surf in, and send forth the Good News, and thereby "give the Internet a soul":

> Without fear we must set sail on the digital sea facing into the deep with the same passion that has governed the ship of the Church for two thousand years . . . we want to qualify ourselves by living in the digital world with a believer's heart, helping to give a soul to the Internet's incessant flow of communication.[2]

The Church and New Media is a book that has looked thoroughly at the "ways and means" of Internet evangelization, and its author Brandon Vogt has sought out a variety of voices—clergymen, church women, laity, converts, and so-called cradle Catholics—who

might be called the "first wave" of what he expects
to be a vital Catholic Internet presence. They are not
only vital but dynamic as well. If the Internet can be
dependably described as a depository for the dusty old
documents of the faith, it is also easy to find within it
the lively depth and breadth of a Church in constant
conversation with the world. Aside from appearing on
social media pages, the Church is present on group
sites and blogs featuring theologians, canon lawyers,
bishops, religious communities, political and cultural
observers, ordained newshounds, cranky writers, and
ordinary priests, moms, dads, young adults, and even
a smattering of teens and tweens. They are not always
agreeing, but all are professing Jesus Christ and his
Church, rejoicing in her seasons, saints, and sacraments,
and sharing in the suffering of its sins.

Recalling Venerable Archbishop Fulton J. Sheen's
seemingly effortless mastery of television back when the
medium was in its infancy, Vogt wrote that "the Church
has consistently been amicable to alternative, emerging
media [and with new media], we call the Church back
to that same orientation. There's nothing here to be
afraid of. The Church has successfully engaged every
past medium and she can do it here, too."[3]

I agree with Vogt, a smart and energetic young man
whom I am honored to call a friend. However, if there
is nothing to be afraid of—and we know this is true
because the angels reassuringly tell it throughout scripture, and Jesus says it in all four gospels—that does not
mean we should let down our guard while participating
in a medium so cunning in its ability to draw us away
from our best intentions and our first focuses—whether

they are to share the faith or simply glean some head-lines. When signing in to the Internet's mesmerizing world-without-borders and venturing forth into the endless mirroring of ourselves and our ideas, we might best protect our perspective (and thus keep the first commandment) by remembering Pope Benedict's 2010 message for the forty-fourth World Communications Day: "The world of digital communication, with its almost limitless expressive capacity, makes us appreciate all the more Saint Paul's exclamation: 'Woe to me if I do not preach the Gospel.'"[4]

The Idols of Coolness and Sex

> Hobbes: "What are you doing?"
>
> Calvin: "Being cool."
>
> Hobbes: "You look more like you're bored."
>
> Calvin: "The world bores you when you're cool."
>
> Hobbes: (Excited) "Look, I brought a sombrero. Now we can both be 'cool.'"
>
> Calvin: "A sombrero? Are you crazy? Cool people don't wear sombreros! Nobody wears sombreros!"
>
> Hobbes: (Deflated) "What fun is being cool if you can't wear a sombrero?"
>
> BILL WATTERSON, *CALVIN AND HOBBES*

Recently Jane Fonda came across my timeline on Twitter. I do not follow her; but someone who did hit the "retweet" button on something she had sent out. Then with each additional tweet, her message moved around the Web until it ended up before my eyes. I don't remember what exactly it was that she had tweeted. If her words were unmemorable, the image she used for her avatar was not. There she was, wearing the shag hairstyle she helped to popularize in the 1970 film *Klute*. Her eyebrows were perfectly plucked and the avatar was raising a fist of solidarity against the establishment. It is an iconic image; but as I looked at it, I wondered why this still-beautiful septuagenarian would prefer to tag her tweets with an image from more than forty years past. Perhaps it is simply her favorite old picture—and people are certainly entitled to show their favorite images of themselves if they want—but why not put up a current image that reveals that seventy-something no longer looks old? Perhaps she simply knows it looks cool. Coolness—an idea of relevancy that goes deeper than mere trends of fashion because it demands constant deconstruction and reinvention—is an idol to which whole generations have willingly bowed and sacrificed.

Do you remember the story I related earlier about the family member who had chosen coolness over getting an education? She eventually grew up and realized there were better, more important things than being cool. Many never do. They become perpetual adolescents who still think they would rather die than be thought out of touch with the *zeitgeist*. They worship at what comedian Flip Wilson used to call "The Church of What's Happening Now," where cynicism replaces an actual creed, the homilies never end, and the sacraments take a serious toll. If Christ and his Church are to be a "sign that will be contradicted" (Lk 2:34), the Church of What's Happening Now is the vehicle of worldly affirmation; its only membership requirement is that one be immediately and unquestioningly in tune with the conventional wisdom of the day (or the week), and against the establishment, as it is continually redefined.

I once asked one of my sons to name three cool people for me, and he answered, "Me, Fonzie, and Tom Waits." I didn't have to ask him why he thought he was cool, and Fonzie is a kind of cultural touchstone of stereotypical coolness; but Waits's specific coolness was a mystery to me. So I asked my son what made him cool.

All he could do was shrug. "He's just cool."

If I ask myself who I would describe as "cool," the answers would be very different; but I would be just as hard pressed in explaining my choices.

There are different degrees and perspectives of cool. I grew up with a lot of Mormons, and their idea of cool was being active in church and tithing a true 10 percent of everything they earned. A friend of mine played piano for an event and made twenty-five dollars; she immediately gave two dollars and fifty cents to her ward.

My Catholic friends and I, on the other hand, thought we were cool because we wore jeans to Mass. The notion of tithing seemed pretty fanatical to us. Other Catholic friends were *so* cool they didn't go to Mass at all. They were too hip and too smart for that old-fashioned stuff. They'd moved beyond it. They were at the height of coolness, the place where coolness becomes unquestioned.

Coolness is one of those things we have difficulty defining; but like pornography, we know it when we see it. I've always thought this little exchange from John Irving's *The World According to Garp* defined it well. When the novel's protagonist, a fledgling writer, submits his first piece and is rejected, he brings the rejection notice to a teacher, wondering about it:

> *"The story is only mildly interesting" [read the rejection], and it does nothing new with language or with form. Thanks for showing it to us, though."*
>
> Garp was puzzled and he showed the rejection to Tinch. Tinch was also puzzled.
>
> "I guess they're interested in n-n-newer fiction." Tinch said.
>
> "What's that?" Garp asked.
>
> Tinch admitted he really didn't know. "The new fiction is interested in language and f-f-form, I guess," Tinch said. "But I don't understand what it's really about. Sometimes it's about it-it-itself, I think," Tinch said.
>
> "About itself?" Garp said.
>
> "It's a sort of fiction about fi-fi-fiction," Tinch told him.[1]

In a similar way, coolness is largely about itself. It is not substantial on its own; rather, it conveys an attitude over substance.

What is behind the drive to be cool? Why does something so ephemeral remain so important to us even after we've left high school and the idea of a cool kids' cafeteria table has been (or should have been) left far

behind? Why do we put such effort into being identified within that number?

I suspect the need to be cool comes from a natural
need to distance ourselves from everything that has
come before, in much the same way that a teenager
instinctively moves to do things differently from her
parents. My baby-boomer generation—shared with
Fonda, although I am a tail-ender—really drove that
instinct to the nth degree. Heaven forbid we should
be like our parents (dubbed "the greatest generation"
by Tom Brokaw) and bow so unquestioningly to forms
of etiquette, cultural norms, government actions, and
Church teachings. Our adolescent self-assertion meant
questioning everything as we searched for ourselves;
and it meant embracing, exploring, and eventually
rejecting most of the new answers, as they whizzed by
like the cars of a super-train.

When we are living in the now, we are constantly
restless and looking for the next thing. We love what is
approaching because it is almost here; once it is here,
we celebrate the now. But it passes quickly, and so does
our interest; and this happens trend after trend, cool
moment after cool moment, until zeitgeist is all that
is left. The spirit of the age and me, and the me-in-
the-now—there is nothing cooler than being able to
embody all that.

Except that, in a way, it's like living in a perpetual
state of Christmas anticipation. We look forward to the
day and as soon as it arrives, we rip open the gifts, break
them quickly, declare ourselves bored, and look for the
next cool thing to come. In this way coolness is sort of
in perpetual service to itself.

Beyond the self-affirmation, though, our pursuit of the outsized notion of coolness has to do with fitting in. Humans are largely social creatures, and our instinctive desire to belong somewhere remains a constant throughout our lives.

It is logical to presume that a sense of security and belonging should be nurtured primarily in the family. If we know where we belong, we know who we are. If we're secure in all of that, then fitting in with the latest idea becomes a minimal concern. Lacking a strong sense of place, however, we seek our identity in the affirmation of others. The idol of times and trends looms large before our awareness; it blocks the unchanging God of eternity, as we give ourselves away to the gratification of now.

I can't help but wonder if some of our instincts to make an idol of coolness have come about thanks to the shakeup of the nuclear family that started in the last half of the twentieth century and is still producing fallout. If the family is the place from which we receive our sense of self and belonging, things became understandably dicey once the parents themselves began adapting the cool standards of their children's generation. From wearing the same clothes as their kids (love beads and bell-bottoms then; jeans and ball caps now), to embracing their ideas, dating habits, and social mores, modern parents have done something rather unprecedented: they've learned from their "enlightened" children and become like them.

Parents abdicating their roles in order to follow their children's sensibilities had a predictably unsettling effect on society. Suddenly everyone was cool, and no one wanted to be the old-fashioned, uptight grownup, except, it seems, the Catholic Church. When Pope Paul VI released *Humanae Vitae*, its message was largely distilled to the public as out of touch: terminally uncool church says "no" to the "now-and-for-ever-cool."[2] The encyclical was summarily ignored by a tuned-in and turned-on populace who accepted that message as delivered by the media, never even bothering to read the encyclical itself. Sin—a very uncool and uptight concept—became a vague notion, one not worth consideration except among the naïve, the primitive, or the terminally hung-up. It was as if the entire world had decided to toss thousands of years of cultural and religious cues to the side and embrace the inner fourteen-year-old. By the time I graduated from high school in the mid-1970s, I was (aside from the Mormon girls) one of the rare virgins in my class. The instinct to deconstruction and the social rejection of everything that came before meant that having sex while in the eighth or ninth grade was cool. Everyone did it, sin was just guilt tripping, and (unless your parents were mean or uncool), if you got pregnant, you just had an abortion. No big whoop. Everything was cool, and if you had a problem with that, you weren't.

One of my classmates—seeking to demonstrate her teenaged feminist *bona fides*, announced when she became pregnant by her twenty-one-year-old boyfriend, her mother was "very cool" with her aborting the baby because her mother had recently had an abortion herself. "It's something we have in common; actually we're more like sisters than mother and daughter."

Perhaps there is something positive to be said about a mother and daughter being able to speak openly to each other about their sex lives—something that might have been unthinkable in previous generations—but her pronouncement gave me the willies. I didn't want to be pals or faux sisters with my mother. And I didn't think I could be comfortable with knowing the life of a sibling of mine had been terminated.

That spirit of contempt for everything that came before is often part and parcel of being cool. A Church of What's Happening Now can have no truck with a God and Church of what was happening then. The new Church must say goodbye to all that old stuff, if it is to serve itself. Several years into our mid-century social upheavals, a large part of being cool still demands an over-focus on religious revisionism, much of it based on sexual issues. The primacy of God is replaced by the primacy of "what I want," most particularly where sex and sexuality are concerned.

Sex, sexuality, and our fascination with our orgasms—both the proclaimed "right"[3] to them and our constant pursuit of that right—have helped to foment the idol we have made of coolness. Because so much of being cool means having sex, we find ourselves condoning all manner of sexual activity and demonstrating complete open-mindedness by recognizing sex as a mostly wholesome recreational activity. Because we see sex that way, it becomes a god of creation completely under our control. After all this time, we're still as intrigued as Eve by the hissing promise that if only we pay no attention to the Creator and his rather spare commands, our own enlightenment will make us his equal. Then we will be beyond needing to listen to God ever again.

I know that in approaching sex this way, I am opening myself up to accusations of prudishness or of being called a sex-hater and simply being dismissed as irrelevant. I'll risk the derision to affirm what the Church has always taught: sex is great. It is also sacred and holy; its creative power, which is essential to God's design, demands that it be respected. When the sexual revolution was making its first inroads, Pope Paul VI tried to warn us what would happen when sexual desires become disconnected from the Creator's plans. *Humanae Vitae* is a brief encyclical; but it's one that, as I mentioned earlier, largely went unread when it was issued. Those who are picking up the encyclical all these years later are discovering this papal discourse on human sexuality and artificial birth control seems more prophetic and more prescient as the decades go by. The human fallout of our idolizing self-interest becomes apparent:

> Responsible men can become more deeply convinced of the truth of the doctrine laid down by the Church on this issue if they reflect on the consequences of methods and plans for artificial birth control. Let them first consider how easily this course of action could open wide the way for marital infidelity and a general lowering of moral standards. Not much experience is needed to be fully aware of human weakness and to understand that human beings—and especially the young, who are so exposed to temptation—need incentives to keep the moral law, and it is an evil thing to make it easy

for them to break that law. Another effect that gives cause for alarm is that a man who grows accustomed to the use of contraceptive methods may forget the reverence due to a woman, and, disregarding her physical and emotional equilibrium, reduce her to being a mere instrument for the satisfaction of his own desires, no longer considering her as his partner whom he should surround with care and affection.

Finally, careful consideration should be given to the danger of this power passing into the hands of those public authorities who care little for the precepts of the moral law. Who will blame a government which in its attempt to resolve the problems affecting an entire country resorts to the same measures as are regarded as lawful by married people in the solution of a particular family difficulty? Who will prevent public authorities from favoring those contraceptive methods which they consider more effective? Should they regard this as necessary, they may even impose their use on everyone. It could well happen, therefore, that when people, either individually or in family or social life, experience the inherent difficulties of the divine law and are determined to avoid them, they may give into the hands of public authorities the power to intervene in the most personal and intimate responsibility of husband and wife.[4]

Perhaps evil's greatest triumph, accomplished long before the sexual revolution, has been to take people's understanding of sex outside of the realm of the spirit and keep it solidly in the camp of the physical. There it is reduced to a few sound bites of personal empowerment, some adolescent giggles, and a few sharp grunts. Sex becomes both earthy and earthbound, without a hint of heaven about it. Calling sex "dirty" might have been an expedient way for parents and societies to address the complex relationship between our sexual and our spiritual natures; but by not unpacking those complexities clearly, openly, and wisely, past generations became complicit in communicating an idea of shame that has fomented neurosis and an inevitable over-correction. Sex went from being something mysteriously sacred to something efficiently nonchalant.

Sex outside of marriage is not sinful (that unpopular, unfair word that makes us feel bad about ourselves) because it is "dirty." It is sinful because, when rendered casual and sterile, the act by which we most closely work with God in creation, the act that takes us into the deepest recesses of our physicality—to our very essences—becomes reduced to nothing more than an end unto itself. Sex is separated from the energetic and spiritual realm in which it is most fully and functionally realized. The sin comes, not because we are bad, but because by our willful action we have removed our emphasis from the spiritual and chained it to the corporeal. We've assisted in the exploitation of ourselves and of others. We've made a good job of keeping our minds, hands, and eyes on our burnished idols and away from God.

If a beautiful park is not maintained, if its users are permitted to run amok—with no accountability to authority—the park is quickly a shambles of litter,

weeds, broken equipment, and squalor. It is the same
with our sexuality. By handing it over to our idols of
sterile gratification and coolness, we permit our own
cheapening. We, the children of God's majesty, get
tossed to the rabble, which becomes ourselves.

Not too long ago, I made a shocking discovery.
It should not have been shocking, but I can be slow
on the uptake sometimes. It occurred to me that our
understandings about sex—for millennia upon millennia and throughout various cultures and religious traditions—have been remarkably consistent. Until pretty
recently, sexual continence was understood to be a
good thing: chastity was honorable; virginity was nothing to sneer at; and (here comes the shocking part), it
was more or less understood that the only people on
the planet who were actually supposed to be engaging
in sexual congress were married couples. I wrote about
it at FirstThings.com:

> From a Western perspective, that sounds
> severe, but Eastern religions teach similarly,
> that all are called to sexual continence . . .
> [F]rom a religious perspective, therefore, it
> does seem that in our nation of 300 million
> people, only a distinct minority of about 120
> million (even less, discounting non-sacra-
> mental unions) are meant to be gifted with
> the duty of delight that is the sexual expres-
> sion of love, within marriage.
>
> Why does this Office get all the fun?
> Because, while all offices are equal, the Office
> of Marriage—far from being "for everyone"
> or a simple expression of a mood subject
> to change—is one of especial humility and

sacrifice. The essentials of procreation residing within us are so powerful that unless
one ardently works to prevent it, new life
will come (a recent study found that 54%
of abortions stem from contraception "fail-
ure"[5]). The little bang of sperm and ova
are the microcosmic reflection of the mac-
rocosmic big bang of Creation; co-oper-
ating with God in the continuance of that
creation means humbly accepting—for the
rest of one's life—involvement and responsibility for specific human beings of varied
gifts and challenges. There are no days off; if
you don't like your job, you can't just move
away; you can't re-staff. Parenthood con-
tains moments of surreal bliss countered by
a lifetime of work, self-abnegation, stress, and
anxiety. Besides procreation, sexual tender-
ness in marriage brings a depth of consolation meant to balance out the fullness of that
burden or—for a childless couple—the pain
of longings unfulfilled.[6]

It was a little mind-blowing, putting this together:
The whole world was called to continence (and to discover what was meant to be their vocation—the purpose
for which they were loved into being). Even though, as
a Catholic, I understood that sexual disobedience was
a grave (or mortal) sin, I suppose on some level I had
been conditioned and conformed to the idea that sex
isn't *much* a sin unless it's exploitative. Suddenly I had
to engage my mind and focus my curiosity on something I hadn't seriously thought about in years: the

sexual ideal that was important enough God included it in his commandments.

Very early on in this book, we established that if the first commandment is being kept, the rest of the commandments naturally fall in line, and each commandment after the first directly relates to the first. Adultery and fornication—what we used to call "sins against impurity"—are condemned throughout scripture; and Jesus goes so far as to warn against even entertaining lustful thoughts, because—as the conventional wisdom goes—a thought is a thing, and the lustful thoughts are therefore as grave as the sins themselves (Mt 5:28).

It is a particularly mid-twentieth-century conceit that everything that came before Jane Fonda's generation was either wrong, outdated, or of dubious value—that any idea dating back to the Iron Age cannot possibly speak to this age. That's a pretty narrow-minded and limiting perspective; it discounts the possibility that what came before us had meaning and that we have simply lost touch with it.

Ideas become idols; it is an unstoppable human truth. We make an idol of our sexuality and our sexual appetites. On some level we understand that if we cannot control these appetites, they will control us—and what controls us takes us away from God. But that feels to us like some distant sort of truth we can easily wave off. "If it feels good, do it" has been a powerful idol of distraction. It is one that keeps us from the fullness of his presence in our lives, and thus his astounding, transcendental, and eternal love, because we're too busy chasing a worldly facsimile.

Of course, it is also possible to fixate so strenuously on sexual continence that it too becomes something of an idol. When we consider how devalued virginity has become, we must consider the possibility that we are currently witnessing an overcorrection in response to some cultures—including Christian ones—that have placed oppressive premiums on an intact hymen.

A family member sometimes talks about her father— a first generation Italian-American who was so fixated on the moral reputation of his daughters that he made their (extremely restricted) post-pubescent lives utterly miserable. When I listen to some of the stories, I think, "Why wouldn't any woman resent that behavior and react against it?" Although she is nearly seventy years old, this family member still gets angry when she recalls her father's disrespectful distrust and the eventual rift his obsession caused them. She is angry at the Church, too, which she blames for feeding his obsession by pro- mulgating a shame narrative, when there was a better, deeper, and more beautiful way to discuss sex. "And for what?" she will fume. "For a meaningless bit of tissue."

In truth, it's not so meaningless; but I completely understand why she would think so and why she would resent a preoccupation with virginity that made it seem like yet another kind of idol. Because we are human and we bring everything down to our human under- standing, our ideas of virginity became wrapped up with notions of honor and purity. Virginity—and that "bit of tissue"—have a higher relevance than we know. In a sense, it is part of a modeling of the whole covenantal relationship between Christ and his Church—the bride- groom and the bride.

When God chose the Jews as his own, he required a symbolic (and real) acquiescence—the willing removal of the foreskin of the penis. It would be a sign of their willingness to be completely vulnerable and exposed to God's will for them. He made a covenant with them; he would be their God, and they would be his people, and the deal was sealed in blood. At the shedding of the foreskin, man and God are bonded.

The need to be vulnerable and open to God is part and parcel of having a real relationship with him, just as vulnerability is the necessary component in human relationships. The blood covenant and the need for vulnerability and openness are mirrored in the relationship between a husband and wife. The thin membrane of the hymen, then, is a kind of counterpart to the foreskin. In shedding the foreskin, the Jew becomes openly vulnerable to God. In remaining a virgin until marriage, the woman becomes vulnerable only (but fully) to her husband, and he—in receiving that vulnerability—answers only to her. He gives his deepest self and the sweat of all of his labors to her. It is another blood covenant. At the shedding of that blood, they become, as Jesus said, "one flesh," one entity.

God says, "Be my people," and there is a blood covenant. A man and woman say, "Be mine," and there is a blood covenant. And because we are all slow on the uptake, Christ emphasizes it again, trying to get us to understand. God becomes incarnate and says, "Be opened. I will show you how. I will make myself vulnerable to you. You may have my blood. It is shed for you and for all so that sins may be forgiven."

It is the greatest of the blood covenants because the blood covers and draws into oneness—not to a tribe, nor a mate, but an entire creation—for better or worse. It's the marriage of heaven to earth and God to man. Perhaps once upon a time we understood that, and when we understand it again, the idol of coolness that devalues virginity and the thoughtless surrender to the idol of our orgasms will be corrected. We will no longer be looking for the next cool thing to embrace and serve before moving away in time to jump on the next new thing.

Having begun this chapter with Jane Fonda, it seems appropriate to end with her. It strikes me that her public career has been an embodiment of that pattern of coolness idolatry. When fists of revolution were cool, her fist was raised. When the god of fitness and self-care was ascendant, Fonda's videos were the rubrics of right worship. When prosperity and yuppie corporatism were in vogue, she married one of the most prosperous corporate types in the world. As baby boomers aged and sought reassurance that they are still vital and sexy, Fonda showed up at media events with plunging necklines and slit skirts (admittedly, looking fabulous!); and now that we have reached an era where people are seriously discussing whether there can and should be limits to free speech, her voice is again in-step with that energy[7], with that spirit of the times. The fact that she would use the old "revolutionary Jane" for her Twitter avatar suggests to me that she still self-identifies as anti-establishment even though, by all measures—economically, socially, spiritually, and politically—she is as establishment as it gets. And yet she is still inclined to ride the zeitgeist, to pay homage to the god of being cool.

Her existence has been one of such privilege that I wondered about this seeming lifelong need to belong so completely to the Church of What's Happening Now. So I took a look at her biography and learned that when Fonda was young, her mother committed suicide after battling mental illness. Her father rather hastily remarried, and that marriage ended in divorce.

It's worth repeating: our families are where we receive our first gleanings about who we are and what our place is in time. If we cannot find affirmation in our family—if we are not introduced to the God who affirms us because he loves us—we look for affirmation from the world, and we learn to serve the idols of coolness and sexuality.

If and when we happen to escape that service, we ought not be prideful about it. There is an old saying that got used a lot in the eighties and nineties when the god of self-help was ascendant. It is attributed to everyone from Plato to Nelson Mandela, but its overuse and misattribution does not make it any less true: "Be kind. Everyone you meet is fighting a great battle."

CHAPTER SEVEN

The Idol of Plans

*Mensch tracht, un Gott lacht. (Men plan,
God laughs.)*

YIDDISH PROVERB

How many times have you refused to do something that has come up at the spur of a moment because you have plans, even if the plans are not set in stone? And let's face it, beyond those Ten Commandments, very little in life is really set in stone.

I recall a house-proud neighbor telling me once that after her husband had had a stroke, from which he thankfully recovered, she had to reassess her ways and learn to bend a little in her routines and plans. "Now, if he asks me to take a walk with him, I drop what I'm doing—I'll even leave the dishes in the sink—and go walking!"

That might not sound like much, but her daily plans included single-handedly maintaining an immaculate house. Dirty dishes in the sink suggested untenable

squalor to her. But caring for her husband had taught
her a lesson: her house had become something of
an idol—the meticulously clean rooms were where
she found her identity, and they reflected something
back to her and to the world—something she wanted
people to see. When life threw something new at
her, though—something involving a person she truly
loved, not merely a person to whom she wanted to
appear bright and shiny—she had to choose. She had
to choose between the idol and real love, real life. She
chose wisely. Her house was still terrifyingly clean most
days, but it no longer possessed her, and her days no
longer revolved around what chore she had planned.
Once her husband convinced her to spend unplanned
hours playing chess with him, her yard even got a little
weedy. When he passed away, she did not regret a single
dandelion; they were evidence of her better choices.

A priest friend of mine taught me a similar lesson. A
few years ago on a Sunday in Advent, he gave one of
the best, most enlightening, instructive, and challenging homilies I'd ever heard. It was fresh and engaging,
and at its conclusion the congregation broke out into
spontaneous applause.

Readers who are Catholic know that not only is
applause—spontaneous or otherwise—*not* meant to
be a common feature of our liturgies, but there are
precious few homilies that would ever inspire it. This
particular homily, however, had been exceptional, and
it energized and raised the whole liturgy.

When I was planning a retreat a few months later,
I recalled that Sunday and called my friend to ask if I

could use parts of his "Scary John the Baptist" homily for my presentation.

"Oh, yeah. That was a good one," he said, "but I can't give you a copy of it, because I don't have one. I never write out my homilies."

I was surprised. The homily had been so perfectly reasoned and built! "That was extemporaneous?"

"I learned a long time ago," he said, "to just get out of the Holy Spirit's way. I read the scriptures, meditate on them, and just trust that what comes out of my mouth will be useful."

Maybe another way to say that is "Drop the plans, step into the path of the Holy Spirit, unencumbered, and let yourself be used."

A homily put down on paper is a plan, and as with any plan, it has built-in limits. Once you have that paper—once you've made that plan—you feel bound to deliver it, and so you're bound to the page, or the plan, rather than open to where the Spirit might lead. To be inflexible about deviating from the plan is to erect a roadblock, an encumbrance—an idol—and put it in the way of what the Spirit might be trying to do with us and for us.

That doesn't mean we should never write a thing down or never make a plan. Some basic planning is essential to life, and even Christ and the apostles had to plan the Passover meal. But when we see a plan changing, our willingness to step into the path of the intention of the Holy Spirit can tell us a lot about whether we are truly open to God's working in our lives, or whether we've created an idol of our plans and expectations and placed them before God.

No plan should ever become more important than God's plan for us.

A great regret of my life is having been too young and too lacking in confidence to be able to articulate this truth to a friend of mine who had discovered she was pregnant about six months before her wedding. When she told me that she had scheduled an abortion, I tried to dissuade her. "You're going to get married, anyway," I said. "Would it be so bad to have the baby?"

"But all of my plans," she said. Like every bride, she had invested a great deal into those plans—the spring wedding when the azaleas would be in bloom for the pictures, the bikini, and the honeymoon. She had an idea of what those first years in a great apartment would be like. All the parties, all the promise, all the plans that had lived for so long in her psyche it seemed impossible—unthinkable—not to serve them.

She had the abortion, and, six months later, her plans went off without a hitch. She got the weather, the beautiful pictures, the honeymoon, and yes, that first year in the great apartment. There were lots of parties, but when the marriage ended, as it quickly did, none of that ended up mattering.

My friend and I are no longer in touch, but I often think about that child—who would be more than thirty years old now, much older than we were then. I wonder if she hadn't clung so desperately to her plans, what might have happened. What if she'd said "yes" to what was unexpected, instead of closing off an avenue to love in her life? She could have had all the love that child would have brought into the world—that inexplicable, unconditional love that comes as such a surprising gift.

And who knows whether, by the force of that newly created, unplanned-for love, the marriage itself might not have thrived?

We cannot know that, of course. But a baby is a coming of new love; it is a means by which God, who is love, renews the face of the earth. Anything might build upon it: new life, new love, and a new phase of God's design. But it was thwarted because there were human plans—which could have been changed and which were not written in stone, except by a choice. Such a loss of irreplaceable love! Such a regrettable choice—made from fear, a lack of trust, or perhaps a simple lack of understanding that a new human being, full of love, is so much more of a lasting adventure than a big wedding and a dusty honeymoon album.

I have nothing but compassion in my heart for women who—for whatever reason—have made that choice and rejected that life-enriching, difficult, challenging, and glorious love. I often think the decision to abort is made in fear, and it makes me wish the first scripture verse any of us are taught could be the line from Jeremiah 29:11: "For I know well the plans I have in mind for you, says the Lord, plans for your welfare, not for woe! plans to give you a future full of hope." God is as good as his word.

Saint Teresa of Avila said, "If in all things you seek Jesus, doubtless you will find him." I am sure that's because God is always already seeking us out, looking for the opening by which he can come to us. He is like a lover looking for the thin places in a garden hedge through which he can approach us and woo us with his plans. His plans may not always line up with our own nor will they necessarily come through to our awareness at all, until later.

That's not entirely our fault. Our society over conditions us to plan—to buy into that illusion of personal control, and we do it all the time about everything. Plans begin even before we are born, as parents plan our names and Baptism parties. I know a woman who began planning for her little girl's entrance into preschool before the child had even entered the world. Before my sons were born—before we even knew they were boys—my husband was planning on them attending his all-male prep school, with a comparable school chosen, of course, for the hoped-for daughter.

We started planning and saving for college before the kids were on solid food. We had so many lovely plans. But the boys weren't remotely interested in my husband's school, and the college savings were not nearly enough to keep us from amassing student loans. Nothing went according to the plans. And yet, somehow—and I truly believe it is because we were willing to let go of our own ideas and be open to other possibilities—things worked out exactly as they should have. Had the school plans survived, one son would not have met his bride. Had he not acquired a bit of college debt, he might never have disciplined his bohemian inclinations into a steady job and career. Had our plans for our other son worked out, he might have been much less happy than he is.

There is a paradoxical kind of power in being willing to sweep away the idols we make of our plans. When Saint Paul writes that "for when I am weak, then I am strong" (2 Cor 12:10), he is telling us when he

surrenders the notion that he could accomplish anything on his own, he discovers that God, working
through him, does wonders beyond his own meager
imaginings. It is precisely the same with our plans.
When we stop insisting upon them and permit God
to throw us a curve, and answer it with trust, wonders
come our way.

Saint Julian of Norwich, in her "shewings"—her
mystical lessons from within the light of Christ—wrote
that we might trust God's plans. They are committed to
our welfare, no matter how difficult, even dire, things
may seem: "All shall be well, and all shall be well, and
all manner of things shall be well."

Saint Paul put it more plainly:

> We know that all things work for good for
> those who love God, who are called accord-
> ing to his purpose. For those he foreknew
> he also predestined to be conformed to the
> image of his Son, so that he might be the
> firstborn among many brothers. And those
> he predestined he also called; and those he
> called he also justified; and those he justified
> he also glorified. What then shall we say to
> this? If God is for us, who can be against us?
> (Rom 8:28–31)

Perhaps we Christians are not teaching it well
enough, either rhetorically or through the examples of
trust we set by how we live our lives. How well are we
reflecting this truth that God wants only what is good
for us, and that if we only trust—the very hardest thing
because it involves a willing surrender of our own sense
of control—then our lives will be richer for it.

I once had an e-mail debate with a regular reader of my blog, a Protestant gentleman who could not comprehend the Catholic Church's teaching on contraception. He understood the idea of always being open to the transmission of life, but he had a different take on what that meant. "My wife and I have our family and our future mapped out," he wrote. "We know precisely what we will be able to afford and how many children we will be able to handle. Does the Church know better than we, what we can handle?"

I teased back, "Do you know better than God what you can handle?"

"Very clever," he answered. "I don't agree that using a condom or spermicide actively precludes God's involvement. He can and has intervened in that way, many times. If he wants us to have another baby, these obstacles are not really obstacles at all!"

So then, I wondered, is the idea of being in control an acknowledged illusion, and is the whole issue a game?

The gent added that because he was, in fact, open to life, if his wife became pregnant while using a condom they would, of course, take this as God's will for their lives. Remembering friends of mine who credit two of their sons to contraception, I said, "Well, chances are you probably will get pregnant at some point then, but that's a heck of a battle plan you've put into place."

This offended my correspondent who insisted he was not at war with God but was simply being responsible. "Of course it's war," I wrote back. "You're saying to God, 'I'm building up battlements, and if you can overrun them, the castle is yours; but if you can't, I win.'"

"It's not about winning or losing," he said.

"You're right," I agreed. "It's about making an offer of your surrender and not attaching conditions or negotiating a treaty. How inspired would you be if your bible read: "And while at Gethsemane Jesus prayed, 'Nevertheless, not my will, but (if the soldiers can catch me) thine be done.' And thus slipping on his Air River Jordans he raced from the garden saying 'Feet, don't faileth me now'"?

Plans that we hold too dearly to do not give God room to operate in our lives. They clutter us up and create blockades to the most primal part of our inmost being—the part where God speaks and through which (if the barricades are down and the lines are open) the divine plan may show itself. What is the lesson then? When making plans, include within them a willingness to bend into the curve of the Holy Spirit, rather than resisting. Things have a way of working out when God is given straight access to our lives and our hearts. As William Blake writes,

> He who binds himself to a joy
> Does the winged life destroy.
> But he who kisses the joy as it flies
> Lives in eternity's sunrise.[1]

CHAPTER**EIGHT**

The Super Idols

When you choose anything, you reject everything else.

G. K. Chesterton

Perhaps because I have not worn a wristwatch in more than thirty years, I have a very good sense of time. My younger son has not made his peace with this reality and will sometimes test me, demanding to know, "What time is it right now?" A few years ago, during a theater performance, he leaned over three times to hiss, "What time is it now?" and after each answer, he would peek at his own watch and lean back in his chair in frustration. At play's end, as we rose, he said, "Really quick, right now, what time is it *exactly*?" and I answered, "Nine twenty-six." From the row behind us a man consulted his watch and announced, "On the button!" Then he leaned in to my son and said, "Your mother is spooky."

"A couple of centuries ago," my husband teased me about my time-telling prowess, "the world would have called you a witch and burned you at the stake." In fact I am neither a witch nor spooky and have long suspected that my ability to accurately judge time has simply been a necessary adaptation. It is not a difficult thing to gauge how much time has passed from one event to another, and undoubtedly I process cues like sun positions and traffic patterns without even thinking about them.

Yet in the past year or so, it has seemed to me that my inner gears have run haywire. Much of my work involves managing a site with dozens of contributors, and working online has altered my ability to measure time. Now, too many are the days when I hear my husband's key in the door and realize that an entire workday has flown by, and I've not given a thought to fixing our supper. The Internet is all about the constant flow of real-time information and updates, but it catches us up in a kind of moment-by-moment suspense that is, paradoxically, disorienting to our real sense of time. It messes with our unconscious cues. Instead of a newspaper landing at our door at a predictable time, our news is nonstop. Instead of the mailbox snapping shut with reliability, the e-mail just keeps pouring in; and even though the exact time is right there on the corner of our screens, it seems we are all looking up from our monitors with dazed expressions, wondering, "Is it really that late? What day is it again? Really, is the week (or the month) nearly over?"

Perhaps a common sense of time slipping so quickly away is behind the date/time prompts designed into all of our electronics. The camera, the phone, the stereo remote, and the thermostat—all are constantly announcing what time it is. I am surrounded by digital numbers, and yet I am increasingly having little Matthew 25:13 moments when I am unsure, within myself, as to the day, or the hour.

Our obsession with time is odd considering what a construct and illusion it is. But perhaps it becomes less odd when we consider that we are equally obsessed with what is contained *within* time. I don't mean our daily routines and commitments. I mean the stuff that very often distracts us from them—the pop-and-celebrity-plus-politics headlines that constitute the times. That's the stuff upon which we too often build our identities and attach our allegiances—the social fallout from all of our busy structuring.

Bob Dylan sang that "the times, they are a-changin'," and that is natural from generation to generation. However, my sense lately is that both time and the times are moving too quickly for us to wholly keep up and keep track. Just as we look up from our monitors wondering, "Is it really that late?" we look around us and see the common touchstones of every culture being turned on their heads. Suddenly new life is not a blessing but a choice; marriage is unimportant, except as a political cudgel; abundance has become suspect while privation is less a shared enemy but a state to which—if all cannot be rich—most should willingly acquiesce. And why? For the sake of a skewed idea of fairness that says either everyone wins at everything all the time, or no one wins at all. The genuinely impoverished are encouraged toward resentment and envy or offered a choice of syrupy sentiment or condescension. Any of those might help them to cope, but none will help them to rise and escape from their destitution.

When we cannot depend upon a recognizable and accurate representation of the time, we either stop concerning ourselves with it altogether, or we attempt to obsess on how to fix it. When the times seem to fall all out of sense and recognition, either we tune them out and thereafter attend to our own amusements, or we try to correct what we think is not working. We try to get the gears in sync and the face of the world back into an order we can appreciate—one we think we can trust to reflect not simply what is relative, but what is true. And of course, all of our ideas are the right ones, so they must be true.

Trying to control the times, we risk falling into serious trouble. When our theories and our outlooks about the times evolve from philosophies into ideologies, and then ideologies devolve into tribalism, we've taken a step into something deeper than the sort of everyday idols we've explored in previous chapters. If Saint Gregory of Nyssa was correct (and he was) that "ideas lead to idols," I might take his thought a bit further and say that "ideologies lead to super idols."

What I have chosen to call "super idolatry" grows out of ideologies too well watered. A super idol is not one but two steps removed from God. If all idolatries contain elements of self-enthrallment, the enthronement of a collection of our ideologies ramps things up by endowing the ego with a heavy veneer of moral authority. Dress up tribal identifications that accompany one's participation in a party or a movement, determine that the opposition is not merely wrong but evil, and suddenly mere ideas become glittering certainties. These certainties give us permission to hate and tell us our hate is not just reasonable but pure. If simple idolatry blocks our view of God, the super idol—because it is so highly burnished—makes us think we are seeing God in our hatred. A hatred that has been polished and purified through the validation of the super idol paradoxically permits only distorted, funhouse reflections of God, and none at all of the God-in-men.

Our ideological passions, particularly if they are not balanced with a simple reminder that none of us can ever be wholly right about everything, keep us so enthralled that we begin to measure every headline, every news story, every sermon, every comment and tweet that comes our way by how it conforms to our worldview. Times, trends, and movements become warped, and to lose oneself in them is to lose sight of God who is unfading reality and beyond time itself. "The cause" becomes so all-enthralling it can easily become the *all* that obscures and—without our intending or perceiving it—takes the place of the One who is all-in-all.

Some may argue that it is only natural to occasionally become a bit overexcited about civic and social matters. Good citizenship is a virtue, and in order to practice it, after all, one must be informed, passionate, and willing to participate in the process. Well, I agree, but only to a point. Informed participation, it seems to me, is largely a positive thing, while enthrallment becomes something else.

Here is a bit of how I see the difference between civic engagement and enthrallment. It has been my observation that those trudging wearily into a polling place after a day's work, even if they are not particularly excited about the candidates, will exit with a bit more energy after having voted. Similarly jurors may wince upon being selected to hear even a minor court case, but they'll generally perform their duties in a serious and responsible manner. I recall being very young and watching my father run a public meeting among workers considering a move to unionize. I believed, then, that it was the way in which he plowed through parliamentary procedure, making sure that all opinions were fairly heard and respectfully received, that held the gathering so spellbound. Later, I came to realize that, his skills aside, what had made everyone in the room feel enlarged, uplifted, and important was probably the simple act of engagement itself. The Reverend Doctor Martin Luther King Jr. famously said, "You don't have to have a college degree to serve. You don't have to make your subject and verb agree to serve. . . . You only need a heart full of grace."[1] Informed participation in civic processes, whether on a jury, at a public hearing, or in the voting booth, instills a sense of pride in service to our communities; it communicates to our neighbors that everyone matters, not just the elite; it reassures us that our small contributions are vital, and our destinies are still our own to chart.

Engagement with "a heart full of grace" is not enthrallment. Enthrallment may engage the heart, but it lacks grace. When we lose sight of the great and Almighty because of our passionate engagement with an earthly cause—and even the most worthy fight in the interests of heaven has its earthly measure—we can also, with astonishing swiftness, lose sight of the inherent dignity of the human person. We can begin to think of the person as "other." Specifically, we lose the willingness to bear with the imperfect, flawed, and sinful humanity of another in light of our own broken propensity to sin. We lose the willingness to "bear with one another" as Saint Paul writes, just as the Lord bears with us. Rather than instructing and admonishing each other "in all wisdom" (Col 3:16), we become incapable of tempering our condemnation with enough mercy to leave room for the Holy Spirit to work either on them or us. And when that happens, we slip into the clutches of the super idol, which steals from us our own humanity.

Ironically, that spiritually deforming hatred is very often conceived in love. We love our country; we love our community; we love our church; we love our traditions; we love our perception of ourselves; we love life; and we love babies. Because we love these things, we are willing to engage in activities that support them. Sometimes, perhaps because of pure commitment to a calling (or perhaps because we love our perception of ourselves loving these things), we become fully enthralled activists with our perspectives so narrowed that little room is left for give-and-take. Our blinders cut off our peripheral vision until mercy becomes invisible; there is only room for battle.

The evidence of my own e-mail bears this out. Over the years, I have received missives from a very illiberal liberal ranting, "You are not human to me!" and from a conservative purist on a purging jag demanding that I either fall in line with their issue du jour or stop calling myself "a conservative"—which, in fact, I never had. When Betty Ford died, I opened my e-mail to find this message from a woman very involved with the pro-life movement:

> While I empathize with the loss Betty Ford's family and friends must be feeling at her death, I do not lament the passing of any unrepentant leader of the pro-abortion movement, bluntly speaking. The world is a safer place for children with one less person facilitating their murders.

Well. Upon reading it, my first thought was that false empathy combined with stridency does much more to hurt the pro-life movement than to help it.

My second was that perhaps the hate mail I have received from people declaring that "Christians idolize the fetus" had a tiny germ of a point after all. This message seemed to me to be an almost inhuman pronouncement, made all the more shocking in coming from a Christian. Taking into account nothing of Mrs. Ford's life beyond her pro-choice stance, the statement was so narrow in focus, so lacking in the hope for mercy that it came perilously close to suggesting three abhorrent, perhaps heretical ideas:

- The complex totality of a human being's life is meaningless.
- Reducing the worth of human beings to their (often poorly thought out) political positions is acceptable.

- The death of an ideological opponent can be shrugged off for the cause, whatever the cause may be.

If given credence, what a dreadful world and awful times these three ideas would bequeath to the very children this pro-lifer works to protect.

The fetus, in this circumstance, is not the idol; the cause is, and since an idol is all about distortion and untruth, the statement by this life-defending woman ultimately does nothing but destroy. With a message deficient in mercy, she has added to the construction of an extremist caricature than can only defeat her own purposes. She has reduced the Church's extremely nuanced and reasonable teachings about human life, the nature of sin, human understanding, and God's mysterious ways and means, to a stark and hardhearted pronouncement that—in a profoundly ironic way—stripped Mrs. Ford, the pro-lifer herself, and her whole movement of precisely that dignity of the human person to which she says she is devoted. Further and most troubling, in pronouncing her judgment upon Mrs. Ford, she usurps God, taking on his role as dispenser of justice while reflecting none of his mercy.

In fairness, I do not think the pro-life advocate's conscious intention was to dehumanize Mrs. Ford or to misrepresent God or life or sin or mercy. I think she was simply so caught up in what she was doing (and perhaps in feeding her media enterprise) that she was thoughtless and working on autopilot. She did not call on all she does know about her faith, about her own sinfulness, her own imperfect understanding, and the mercy of God, before she hit the send button.

We all do that from time to time; we get caught up in our cause, and we become careless with our words. Sometimes that's about busyness and distraction, and not idolatry. But when we catch ourselves being thoughtless (or when someone points it out to us), we should consider the first commandment and ask ourselves if we have not elevated the object of our enthrallment to that position where it blocks God.

A good way to tell if God is being blocked is if we have lost sight of the hope for mercy for the sake of another. Justice matters, of course, but as Saint Paul reminds us in Romans and Hebrews, God said "The Lord shall do justice for his people." (Dt 32:36) By contrast, Christ's example on the cross reminds us that mercy is ours to bestow upon each other.

The essayist Annie Lamott has an even easier way to discern whether we have slipped into idolatry, which, you'll recall, is always rooted in our fascination with ourselves: "You can safely assume you've created God in your own image," she wrote, "when it turns out that God hates all the same people you do."[2]

In my introduction I related that I could be boisterous in defense of a president I judged to be unfairly reviled, until I became concerned that my instinct to defend was leading to kneejerk approvals of policies I would find objectionable in another president. This revelation led to my first awareness that ideology could easily trip us into an unthinking idolatry.

Recent studies seem to indicate that political identities are becoming more entrenched, and passionate ideologues are much less willing to engage in compromise with the opposition or within the disparate ranks of their own allies. For Christians, this is a dangerous business. If we begin to conflate our religious interests with political and social ones, we can damage the Body of Christ. We do this by yielding to the temptation—thanks to the super idol—of condescension, whereby we identify some Christians as the "right" sort, worthy of our friendship and prayerful support, and others as the obstinate "wrong" sort, whom we judge worthy only of our wrathful correction.

When Anne Rice announced that she was quitting Christianity, but not Christ—abandoning organized Christian churches in general, the Catholic Church in particular, and an identifier or label that was problematic to her politics—she was doing something similar. She was roiling the Body of Christ by proclaiming it so infested and hate ridden that the "better elements" of Christianity must be compelled to jump from it.

> I'm out. In the name of Christ, I refuse to be anti-gay. I refuse to be anti-feminist. I refuse to be anti-artificial birth control. I refuse to be anti-Democrat. I refuse to be anti-secular humanism. I refuse to be anti-science. I refuse to be anti-life. In the name of Christ, I quit Christianity and being Christian . . . following Christ does not mean following His followers. Christ is infinitely more important than Christianity and always will be, no matter what Christianity is, has been or might become.[3]

I have difficulty believing that anyone who has read *Humanae Vitae* or the documents of the Second Vatican Council, or who has paid attention to Christianity's

contributions to scientific research can credibly con-
demn the Church as anti-female, anti-human, or anti-
science. Rice essentially has proclaimed that she wants
to do the life in Christ on her own, while saying yes to
the world and its values. She misses the simple truth
(and our emptying pews suggest she is not alone in this)
that far from being an institution of no, the Church is
a giant and eternal urging toward yes to God—whose
ways are not our ways and who draws all to himself,
in the fullness of time—rather than a yes to ourselves.

The continual yes we bestow upon ourselves always
ends up enabling an idol and diminishing others. I
know whereof I speak. When I was a little girl, I used
to watch the pendulum of our big grandfather clock
swing back and forth. I was fascinated by that hovering
nanosecond of suspension at either end, that moment
when the brass circle had swung as far left as it could
go and had no option but to swing back to the right.
There it would reach its culmination and throw left
again. This constant state of flux was necessary in order
to get an accurate reading of the time. A pendulum at
dead center, of course, would mean unproductive stasis;
the clock would be correct only twice a day and then
only for a moment each time. The other twenty-three
hours and fifty-eight minutes would be misrepresenta-
tive and false. Eternal suspension at the extremes or
at dead center—all either can promise is distortions
of reality. True balance, then, requires some regulated
give-and-take if it is to be productive and if its productivity is meant to be authentic.

My political pendulum has swung from the left side
of the spectrum and then to the right. I have visited

both extremes and am ashamed to admit that while my pendulum hung at either end, I—figuratively speaking—had no idea what time it was. I was fully immersed in the distortions, fully enthralled with my passionate engagement. It became all too easy to see those with whom I disagreed as an amorphous "they" upon whom my righteous condemnation could be heaped and whose humanity I easily lost sight of.

If the nation is troubled and if our polarization is stranding us, we must ask whether it's because we are enthralled with our ideas and the ideologies, obscuring God and leaving no room for the Holy Spirit to maneuver. This state of affairs is not unique to our history, though. In his Second Annual Message to Congress in 1862, Abraham Lincoln cut to the heart of the matter: "We must disenthrall ourselves," he said, "and then we shall save our country."[4]

We Christians are not supposed to hide our lights under a bushel basket, and we're also not supposed to glare at others, sending them scurrying back into the shadows. At the Transfiguration, Jesus' dazzling brightness did not sting the eyes of the apostles. A light that is well placed does not repel others; it attracts from out of darkness. Too many of us haul the light of Christ about like a burning cross, seeking to confront "them" and repair the times, believing that political engagement is the perfect impetus for correction. Yes, we become enthralled; we are in danger of erecting super idols.

Increasingly I am coming to realize that the corny old song "Let there be peace on earth, and let it begin with me," is speaking a truth. Pope Benedict XVI has said, "God does not force us to believe in him, but draws us to himself through the truth and goodness of his incarnate Son."[5]

This is for all of us; its truth belies all of the divisions we create and negates all of our excuses. Benedict's words call to the stabilization of all our excesses and the righting of all of our intentions through all times and circumstances. If we want to change the world, we begin there, allowing ourselves to be drawn to Jesus Christ, sitting at the Master's feet and taking his instructions to heart.

The key to the Christian life begins with confronting and amending the self, rather than indulging it. This can only be done through grace, which enters upon our yes and moves and grows on the intentional breeze of willingness. Because those are the only things that count—our intentions and our willingness—worthiness does not enter in.

But willingness only comes with humility. It comes when we can say, "Thy will be done," and then actually surrender, instead of preparing a treaty, complete with expiration date.

Such surrender is the ultimate disenthrallment and the banisher of all idols, even the super idols.

Through the Looking Glass: Super Idols and Language

> "I don't know what you mean by 'glory,'" Alice said.
>
> Humpty Dumpty smiled contemptuously. "Of course you don't—till I tell you. I meant 'there's a nice knock-down argument for you!'"
>
> "But 'glory' doesn't mean 'a nice knock-down argument,'" Alice objected.
>
> "When I use a word," Humpty Dumpty said in rather a scornful tone, "it means just what I choose it to mean—neither more nor less."
>
> "The question is," said Alice, "whether you can make words mean so many different things."
>
> "The question is," said Humpty Dumpty, "which is to be master— that's all."
>
> LEWIS CARROLL, *THROUGH THE LOOKING GLASS*

G. K. Chesterton delighted in paradox, and so it is not surprising that he delighted in God. The Christ who taught us about saving one's life by losing it, or becoming the servant in order to become the master, shows us the paradox of God by his very Incarnation. The Creator of all condescends to become the most helpless and vulnerable of creatures in order to save and complete them.

Loving both freedom and paradox, Chesterton argued for the beauty of the Ten Commandments, seeing in them not a world full of no, but of yes. He wrote that "the curtness of the Ten Commandments is an evidence, not of the gloom and narrowness of a religion, but . . . of its liberality and humanity [because] most things are permitted."[1]

We are so conditioned to think of religion as being a bunch of rules—of the commandments as being a sometimes sensible, sometimes irrelevant, sometimes annoying list of restrictions—that Chesterton's words almost seem absurd. But Chesterton was correct. There is nothing wider than God's mercy or deeper than his love, if we consent to bend to him, rather than toward our own inclinations. From where we stand, however, we may easily miss this insight. It seems too simple, and we super-bright twenty-first-century beings are living in a very complicated place.

In the previous chapter, when discussing the concept of the super idol, I wrote, "A hatred that has been polished and purified through the validation of the super idol paradoxically permits only distorted, funhouse reflections of God, and none at all of the God-in-men." If our ideological enthrallments make us aggressive in our doubts, fierce in our judgments, and all too willing to set our own ideas in stone (like commandments from on high) until we are imprisoned within them, there is yet another side to that super idol. It is the side that tempts us to think too well of ourselves to ever make a judgment at all, except upon those who dare to judge others—something that we, of course, would never do.

What? That doesn't make sense to you? I said we were in a complex place—one complicated not by paradoxes but perturbation.

Welcome to the other side of the super idol, which we access by slipping, like Alice, past the funhouse mirrors that have already skewed our perceptions of God and the world. We've moved beyond all that, landing in a place where simple words and ordinary virtues have become so complicated that good faith cannot be safely assumed (unless the thinking of others conforms to our own). In that place, we think very well of ourselves indeed. We are in a place of deep cynicism, but that is rarely acknowledged, because so many of us residing within this disordered idol's shadow confuse cynicism with cleverness. Similarly, we confuse love with hate, silence with peace, narrowness with breadth, and we do this mostly because everything is relative in this place.

Through prolonged idolatry, we now inhabit a place that is beyond God, or at least beyond establishment understandings of God; we've crossed into a wavy subjectivity that seems at first to be wise, open, and limitless. This subjectivity is unbound by the strictures of any commandments beyond our own and bent to shape our personal truths, which are not subject to anyone else's moralizing judgment.

Being on the tail end of the baby boom, I grew up at a time where, seemingly overnight, two important and complicated words—*love* and *peace*—became graffiti and poster art and syllables to babble when one had nothing else to say. My classmates and I would scrawl "peace" and "love" on our blue binders in a mindless, hazy way. We didn't know why we were writing those words; but everyone else was using them, selling them, and wearing them, so we did too.

During that time, the word *love*—a deep word communicating all kinds of messages about permanence, commitment, self-abnegation, and sacrifice—began to be used to describe situations and encounters that were shallow, short-lived, casual, and self-serving. Simultaneously, the word *peace*, an equally deep word that, especially when partnered with *love*, gets to the heart of contentment, serenity, gratitude, and joy, was hauled into the shallows, where it came to mean mostly an "absence of war" and nonjudgmental permissiveness. The irony escapes many, but *peace* and *love* were the pretty-but-empty, wallpapery buzzwords that framed an era of riot and social revolution that is still resonating within our society. Cultural and religious disorder has reigned ever since.

If we have nothing to say, then I guess those words are probably preferable to anything else we might utter; and in truth, *peace* and *love*, either conceptualized or spoken, if applied at critical moments, can do the work of God and the angels. Overused, misapplied, or simply bandied about, they become as meaningless as scrap paper; and when we render words meaningless—especially powerful words like *peace* and *love*—our understanding of them becomes warped. Then, as when a teenager flings his stuff thoughtlessly and lazily about the house—disorder follows.

People die for the depth of feeling and understanding that reside within *peace* and *love* when they are rightly defined. When the meaning of these words is up for grabs, so are the chances that anyone would think of sacrificing himself (or herself) for amorphous relativism. And when sacrifice is removed from the equation, an unpromising future of sterile self-regard is what remains.

If *love* and *peace* have been rendered meaningless due to overuse and misuse, *sacrifice* comes by its meaninglessness through disuse. It's not a word we hear much in the secular or sacred world. We talk about Christ's sacrifice, of course, and the word gets hauled out at Lent; but otherwise it's a word mostly heard at Memorial Day observances.

There was one occasion when the word came my way, quite unexpectedly, from a public-school teacher. In their elementary years, my sons always enjoyed the annual science fair. They never won, but they enjoyed coming up with unusual demonstrations; and once in a while, to their great delight, they would find an "honorable mention" ribbon on their display. One year, there was no announcement of an upcoming fair, and so during a conference with a teacher, I asked about it. "No more science fairs," he said. "They're out."

It seems a minor donnybrook had occurred during one of the (admittedly many) parent/teacher meetings I had missed. Parents liked kids getting awards for their work. Teachers felt bad because some kids

were routinely singled out for public praise while others never got any. The teachers wanted to give participation ribbons for everyone entered in the fair. The
parents (perhaps because their mantels were already
full-to-busting with participation certificates that meant
nothing more than "I was there and did this") were
not interested in finding a spot for yet another vague
trophy. The parents thought only outstanding work in
science should be recognized as such.

Absolutely convinced of the rightness of their respective causes, neither side would budge; and so, in order
to prevent having this debate every year, the science
fair was simply cancelled, forever. That, the teacher told
me, was deemed the best, most fair, and most expedient
solution to the problem; and "I hope the honor roll
goes next," he said.

"What's the matter with the honor roll?" I asked.

Essentially the same thing. Some kids always made
the honor roll; some kids never made it; and some kids
made too big a deal when they managed to make it one
semester, only to be crushed if they missed inclusion
the next.

"But the honor roll is an incentive," I said. "If a kid
really wants to be on it, he'll work harder to get there.
Work hard and reap the benefit; it's a good life lesson."

"Except some kids work harder but never get there,
and then they feel bad about themselves," the teacher
said.

"And that's another good life lesson," I countered,
"that sometimes you work hard, and things don't quite
work out as you'd hoped. It's how we learn to buck

it up and grow fortitude. So you don't feel bad about yourself and wallow in it."

He signaled his rejection of that perspective with a little snort that I took to be derision. Obviously I was either a cockeyed optimist (which meant my intelligence was suspect) or I wholly lacked compassion. I was neither stupid nor unsympathetic; I simply thought "sometimes you fail" was ultimately a much better lesson than "nobody succeeds" or "everybody wins."

"But if there is no incentive, no reason to strive for excellence, even if it's just to find your name on a roll," I asked, "aren't we encouraging mediocrity?"

He said, "We're teaching kids to sacrifice the gratification of standing out, for the sake of everyone."

"A sacrifice is something voluntary," I argued. "If you take something away from kids that they want, you can't call it a sacrifice. It's a removal. One cannot sacrifice what one has no opportunity to actually have. And why is the school teaching about sacrifice anyway?"

I was still shooting questions as my husband led me away.

So, *sacrifice*, at least in some corners, no longer has anything to do with voluntary self-denuding or the opening up of oneself to what is difficult. It is about being told no and sitting back down.

Gosh, and some people say religion is narrow and repressive!

So the school had taken it upon itself both to redefine the word *sacrifice* and teach its erroneous concept to its students. And it had also decided to spread the message that everyone was a special individual, so special that not one of them stood out from the rest, or should want to. Delivered in a secular and government-run environment, it's a strange, disordered, almost non-sensical message, isn't it? Everyone is special? Special to whom besides family? Special by what measure if everyone is the same? This seems a concept better suited to a church—in any tradition—than to a school, doesn't it? Within a religious system of belief (one able to recognize a creator and reference something greater than self), a sensible, convincing, and therefore meaningful case can be made that every person truly is special to God who loved them into being, with all of their accompanying gifts and weaknesses. They are special to God who calls them each by name and has counted every hair on their heads, so that—even if they never win a science fair or make an honor roll, even if no one but their mom ever sees them as anything special—their true uniqueness is obvious to God.

The same goes for the word *sacrifice*, actually. In a church setting, we can make a sacrifice of something we are not even permitted to have. We can do it spiritually, and it's called "offering it up." In a school setting, to what being or entity would such a spiritual offering be made?

The offering would be made to an idol of some sort, obviously, an idol belonging to a secular tribe—the same tribe that took *love* and *peace*, emptied them of mystery and filled them back up with meaninglessness.

So, here we are, on the other side of the super idol, having slipped through the funhouse mirrors of our idolatry. We are strangers in this strangest of lands, clueless, yet highly motivated by our own imaginings. We barely notice what it means to move beyond God (hint:

our backs are now to him) or how deficient we are in understanding the nature of love. We pronounce— much like a cab driver I knew in Rome—that what is behind us does not matter. "Nonessential," we say. "The world back then is not the world today. Today we are enlightened; all we need is love, and love is sensitivity, and love is all we need."

We need to reclaim all of the words we're seeing redefined, for the sake of honesty and reality; but of all of them, it is imperative that we reclaim the word *love*. In the First Letter of John, we read, "God is love" (1 Jn 4:8). We can believe this because both love and God share the dual and paradoxical characteristics of complexity and simplicity, accessibility and unfathomability. We can never fully grasp either—the void that has resided within each of us since Eden makes it so.

God is love. Trying to separate those two ideas— chasing God without love or love without God—can lead only to error. We pursue both imperfectly, often by following our hunches or our hearts and steadfastly refusing the established tools and vehicles God has given us for use in the journey. Here on the other side of the super idol, this is especially true. We no longer have our strange gods before God (or between us), which means we might yet connect with the Creator and his will. We believe we are forging a new path to something good, without stopping to consider that the word *good* comes from God who, by the way, is love.

Slipping further through the density, we forget the primary teaching of Christ—to first love God with all our heart, mind, and soul, and then love others as ourselves (because, as the saints have illustrated for us throughout the ages, that's how it works). Instead we take it backward, starting with ourselves and stating with certainty and a little annoyance, that if everyone would "just be more loving" like Jesus was, the God thing would take care of itself.

From there, having claimed the distinction of already being pretty loving people—that better element of Christianity—we endeavor to map out how we can make ourselves love more (as though love can be legislated or taught in school), and make everyone else do it too.

We start out by earnestly and endlessly promoting notions of tolerance and compassion and justice and mercy, and then stretch their boundaries until the words, unsurprisingly, become detached from their meaning.

My elders taught me to live and let live, which is how they defined tolerance. If they said, "Walk a mile in his shoes," it was to plant some empathy and compassion within my forming conscience. They knew me for a little fiend who needed lessons in manners and social etiquette, but they also understood their own limitations. All they could do was teach me by word and example and hope the lessons held. They could not compel me to forbear or to empathize or to love. If my virtues were to have any meaning, I had to engage in them freely. Compassion under compulsion is empty and void.

Still, tolerance and compassion and justice and mercy are worthy things, and we should certainly practice them in our daily lives. Indeed, Jesus' command to "love your neighbor as yourself" is an invitation to embrace such practices. We cannot wholly obey Christ without them. That being the case, what sort of person would dare dispute with people who are only trying to follow the examples of the tolerant, compassionate, just, and merciful Christ? And what if those people seem to be moving the concepts beyond Jesus' actual teachings, which, as it turns out, were simply not as comprehensive as Jesus made them seem? What sort of creepy, sick person says no to an expansion of humanity being more loving?

That clever question, of course, is asked from the back altar of that super idol, and it is one that intimidates people into a swift acquiescence to subjectivity. People will suspend critical thinking or simply embrace silence, rather than admit to a discomfort among all that expanded meaning; they'll tumble into relativism rather than risk expulsion from their respective folds. When we get wrapped up in this side of the enthrallment idol, we succumb to passive-aggression way, and learn to wield it upon others.

Human beings are social animals. Most of us want to fit in somewhere; and no one wants to be thought of as cold, unfeeling, or mean. Often those who are instinctively broad-minded and who find it quite natural to accept others as they are will resist when they perceive that a word like *tolerate* has become so elastic it actually means, "Bestow your unstinting approval on this idea, or you are awful."

"Wait, no, I'm not awful," they will insist. "I don't hate this special-interest group. I just think realities are being ignored and justice . . ."

"You talk about justice," the better elements will jeer, "but what about mercy, huh?"

"You're always ranting about mercy," they sputter back, "but justice leads to it! They go together!"

The battle rages, and tolerance falls by the wayside.

Justice and mercy are the right and left sides of the horizontal beam of the crucifix, upon which a near-constant tug of war ensues. Pro-justice tugs right, and pro-mercy tugs left, again and again. They both move farther away from each other and away from Christ, the centering balance who is all justice and all mercy.

No wonder we become disoriented. The battle ensues, and whichever side possesses the ability to destructively label and defame an opponent to his peers has the edge. Eventually the one or the other will either abandon the war for the enthrallment side of the super idol (reluctantly doubling down on the ideology out of a sense of self-preservation) or will simply give in. Some will surrender on a difficult issue because—despite their own gut feelings, studies or common-sense argument that says even forbearance has limits if it is lived in truth—their friends are telling them otherwise, and the idol of belonging must be served. In the end, they find it easier to forget about scripture, tradition, and natural law; they go along to get along. They bring their thoughts into social alignment, rather than lose associations or risk hearing they are intolerant or have no compassion in a world that has made gods of these virtues.

These virtues are such gods that many of us (in our respective tribes) have, at one time or another, signed on to crusade for them. We have willingly taken sledgehammers to red-hot rhetoric, re-forging words into weapons and then deploying them mercilessly against others until all unloving, doubt-filled thoughts or intolerant questions have ceased, and cowed silence reigns. So that everyone will be more loving, we cry "shame" and wield potent accusations of unfairness and hatred upon those who argue a salient point, even on a subject to which they have averred a general sympathy. In the tussle to insure right thinking, it's all or nothing. There is no middle ground. Hardcore dissenters risk having conferred upon them a dreaded (and socially and professionally annihilating) scarlet *-ist*. Depending on which label can do the most damage, they may be tagged a "rac*ist*," "sex*ist*," "age*ist*," "size*ist*," "Christian*ist*," "modern*ist*," "post-modern*ist*," "traditional-*ist*," "social*ist*," "Marx*ist*," and so forth, and be all but abandoned as unclean if they don't pipe down.

The cult of the godlings, tolerance and compassion and justice and mercy (let's call it the cult of the social virtues), was easily constructed and quickly grown because these idols *do* have a connection to the golden rule; and they therefore shine very brightly—the better to watch ourselves as we are being so very virtuous. In service to them, and to further burnish our shining reflections, we offer up as sacrifice the subtle bullying of others through soft tyrannies that sound like mild corrections but do not invite debate. We will never actually say, "Shut up," because to do so would be harshly direct and thus an evidence of our own imperfect love. Instead we take the indirect route to suppressive unkindness by saying:

- "That offends me!"
- "Shush; be nice!"
- "You're not being fair!"
- "Why are you such a bully?"
- "And you call yourself a Christian?"

Interestingly the tentacles of this cult reach into both sacred and secular institutions, and those who adhere to its teachings may use identical language in either venue. If secular society has no use for a believer who dares to inveigh against material (and especially sexual) concupiscence, it throws its arms wide open once we amend our creed and give precedence to the cult of the social virtues. Here the authority of the state has kissed the most correct teachings of the Church, and they have melded into one strategic unit of human control. God really needn't be in the public picture anymore, although private worship would, of course, be put up with for the sake of charity.

Here's the thing, though. We are created with free will. From Mount Sinai, God set before us a rather brief but important guideline and then gave us the freedom to utterly ignore it and him, if we choose to. We can be as intolerant as we want to be, as cold, unjust, and unmerciful as we wish. We may reject all knowledge of God. We may reject every precept because we are free.

Only that which is secure in truth can afford to allow freedom outside of itself. What is not secure, be it an idea or a movement or a social decree, insists on conformity and permits no dissent.

About twenty years ago, even though I was not much for daytime television or trendy movements, I became aware that healing the inner child was a thing people were doing. Authors were writing books on the subject. People who were comfortable with sobbing before audiences helped sell out the speaking tours of pop-psychologists. Every magazine or tabloid had something to recommend to the service of our inner children. Perhaps today I would roll my eyes at it all and think, "You mean, *idolize* the inner child," but at the time, I wasn't leery of idols. And besides, I had glanced at my inner child and discovered she was a hot mess.

I'd suspected it for a while. When I was growing up, my family seemed as messed up as the rest of the households in our neighborhood. To me this meant that a measure of mess was merely normal. It wasn't until I met my husband and his family and made some adult friends (one of whom heard me recount a family story and called it "Dickensian"), that I realized differently. Prompted by this new information (and a surprisingly rage-filled reaction to a Christmas carol one night), I realized that my inner child needed servicing. I found a therapist and starting exploring. My therapist thought the Christmas anger was merely a cover for something else. I doubted it, but—long story short—there came a point where she encouraged me to talk to my surviving family members about a long-lasting sexual abuse situation in my childhood. This was supposed to be a powerfully healing experience, and—because I was more than aware that my siblings had their own wounds—I sincerely hoped we could all take the chance to lay our stuff bare, call "olly, olly, oxen free," and finally exhale together. So I told my family my story. I did it as simply, clearly, and calmly as I could, which—as it turned out—was pretty calm.

Amid all the yelling, oaths, and cursing that ensued, what I chiefly remember of that day is the almost supernatural composure that I felt while being called "mean" and "a liar" and some other, less flattering things. I knew that what I was telling was the truth. I was not relating to my family a recovered memory but one I had lived with for many years. The memory was like a chronic injury that occasionally flared up and made me limp but did not threaten my life.

Because I was secure in the truth, there was no reason for me to insist on being believed or accepted, validated or even loved; and besides, I couldn't make anyone feel a thing they did not want to feel.

When something is true, there is no point in arguing. We cannot make anyone believe anything, which is why I did not argue with my family and why God does not argue, plead, cajole or negotiate with us. He simply tells us, "I am who am" (Ex 3:14) and—because he is truth and thus secure in his "I am"—leaves us free to seek him out when we are ready to know truth. He leaves us free to love him when we are ready to face the enormity of truth in love.

This is not to say that God is passive; his love is a constant that lures and accommodates us in mind-boggling ways. He became incarnate so he might share our lot with us, and he died in order to redeem us. In *Co-Workers of the Truth*, Pope Benedict XVI, then Cardinal Joseph Ratzinger, put it this way:

> It is obvious that God did not intend Israel to have a kingdom. The kingdom was, in fact, a result of Israel's rebellion against God and against his prophets, a defection

from the original will of God. The law was
to be Israel's king, and through the law,
God himself. . . . But Israel was jealous of
the neighboring peoples with their powerful kings. . . . Surprisingly, God yielded to
Israel's obstinacy and so devised a new kind
of kingship for them. The son of David, the
king, is Jesus: in him God entered humanity
and espoused it to himself. . . . God does not
have a fixed plan that he must carry out; on
the contrary, he has many different ways of
finding man and even of turning his wrong
ways into right ways. We can see that, for
instance, in the case of Adam . . . and we
see it again in all the twisted ways of history.
This, then, is God's kingship—a love that is
impregnable and an inventiveness that finds
man by ways that are always new. . . . God's
kingship means that we have an unshakable
confidence. No one has reason to fear or to
capitulate. God can always be found.[2]

If I may take a detour here—because it is important—what sort of God is this? This is the God who
yields to a people who do not understand, and who—
like spoiled adolescents—tell him time and time again
that no, they are not patient enough, not mature
enough, just too darned human to put up with doing
things his way, which is the way of wisdom.

This is remarkable, almost reckless love. This is a
love so all in all, so unconditional, that it is willing not
just to be vulnerable, but by human standards almost
foolish in its boundless, unconditional reality. What
better way can we recapture our understanding of the

true meaning of love than with this example? Look at
the profundity of God's love for his people, Israel, and
for those of us grafted onto that branch. He gives his
people something better than a king—something tran-
scendent and eternal and incorruptible. But because
they are so body-bound, so captive to their senses to
touch, hear, taste, and smell, they cannot see what he
shows, which is everything. And so they whine, "Well,
we want a king like they have over there," and God,
staggeringly, acquiesces.

God takes pity on human limitations and tries
another way of teaching and reaching, a better way to
know the transcendence. He says, in essence,

> My love and my law are not enough? You
> need a corporeal king? All right then, I will
> come down and be your corporeal king. I
> will teach you what I know—that love serves,
> and that a king is a servant—and I will teach
> you how to be a servant in order to share in
> my kingship. In this way, we shall be one—as
> a husband and wife are one—as nearly as this
> may be possible between what is whole and
> holy and what is broken. For your sake, I will
> become broken, too, but in a way meant to
> render you more whole and holy, so that our
> love may be mutual, complete, constantly
> renewed, and alive. I love you so much that I
> will incarnate and surrender myself to you. I
> will enter into you (stubborn, faulty, incom-
> plete you, adored you, the you that can never
> fully know me or love me back), and I will
> give you my whole body. I will give you all of
> myself unto my very blood, and then it will

finally be consummated between us, and you will understand that I have been not just your God but also your lover, your espoused, your bridegroom. Come to me, and let me love you. Be my bride; accept your bridegroom and let the scent and sense of our love course over and through the whole world through the church I beget to you. I am your God; you are my people. I am your bridegroom; you are my bride. This is the great love story, the great intercourse, the great espousal, and you cannot imagine where I mean to take you, if you will only be faithful . . . as I am always faithful, because I am unchanging truth and constant love.

This God of Abraham, this king, this one who ravishes will give us anything, if we only are willing to trust the truth, even though we do not understand—have not understood since humanity first showed its instinct to hide from God, and will never fully understand—what it is his love has in mind for us, which is simply, "Olly, olly, oxen free; in my light, in my love, you need not hide."

The strain of our brokenness, however, strands us forever in Eden, trying to manipulate truth to what we think is our advantage and—because we know we're doing so—hiding, utterly afraid of authentic love, and, therefore, open to reasonable reproductions and idols.

For my siblings, twenty-some years ago, it was just the same. They did not want the truth. They wanted a lie that would support an illusion that everything was fine. When I could offer only the truth, they tried to shield themselves from me and go into hiding. They knew they were—in their brokenness—embracing a lie, and that made them afraid too, because they did not know that my own love had "olly, olly, oxen free" in mind.

Before they hid, though, and solely because they could not be secure in their subjective, insistent, and unacquainted-with-reality "truth" (and therefore could not afford me freedom outside of it), they made one last attempt to bully me into submission. They wanted to browbeat me into resurrecting that illusory "fine, everybody be nice" state—that idyllic idol meant to better reflect their feelings. They tried to say, "Shut up," with sentences strikingly similar to the ones used by the cult of the social virtues: "You are offensive. You are mean. You are a bully. You are unjust. You are a bad Christian because you have no tolerance and no compassion. Where is your mercy?"

In fact, I had a great deal of compassion for the man who hurt me, and plenty of mercy because I was tolerant enough—and just enough—to consider his own frustrated, powerless life, and to understand that his sickness was conceived in the hellhole of his own Dickensian childhood. Pondering all that, I could even feel pity. I could forgive him, but I could not change what was true so that it became untrue. I could not and would not trade reality for a polite fiction—inauthentic, but convenient for others. I was none of the things my siblings called me, but they needed the accusations in order to give distance. They needed to label me in order to feel safe. They needed the judgments in order to feel justified in hate, which led them idol-bound, seeking reflected-back rays of righteousness until it felt almost like love—like they fit in, somewhere.

A hate that feels like love, of course, is one of those sub-idols that clears the path for the super idol. In this case, the idol is the one that helps us to think well of ourselves when we are thinking poorly of those who refuse to conform to polite fictions, so that we might anchor the idols more securely.

"Hatred," says psychologist Robert Enright, "has a long shelf life. Once it enters into the human heart, it's hard to get it out. It breeds destruction, discouragement, and hopelessness."[3] In the cult of the social virtues, we see what happens when noble ideas mutate into idols; and the tribal efforts to make people more loving and right thinking (by compelling their obedient conformity) become animosity made righteous.

Anyone who has ever been targeted by a pack of bullies (or has run with one) understands that when we are venting hatred along with others, we acquire a sense of belonging and purpose that—quite unlike love—comes to us in an expeditious and rather painless way. Mob-supported (or legislation-supported) suppression of the other removes openness from the social equation; and that, in turn, takes away vulnerability, leaving us with a powerful sense of communal well-being. We love our hate because it makes us feel beloved and invited to the party. We no longer have to think for ourselves.[4] To continue to fit in, all you need is hate, and hate is much easier to entertain than love; it requires so little of us.

This hate that feels like wide-open love is, paradoxically, limiting and self-defeating. Once hatred has become our social vehicle of choice, the travel options become limited: either stay the course and wear the blinders or attempt to break free of the tribe and risk the very real possibility of wearing a scarlet *-ist* of our own.

Regardless of whether we hate a Republican governor or a pro-abortion president or Hollywood or fundamentalism or the system or even a sports team, if our sense of belonging depends on that hatred, then second thoughts will flee, and stagnation will follow. The only way to reenergize and delay the inevitable endgame described by Enright as "destruction, discouragement, and hopelessness" is to find a new hate to love. There must always be an Orwellian subject of revilement—an Emmanuel Goldstein toward whom we can direct a ready and visceral hatred so our facsimile of love can feel fresh and new.

The most insidious part of this hate collective is how easily we can slip into its influence through the simple error of attaching real but disproportionate feelings of love onto things which are often ultimately meaningless: I love my politics so much I must hate you for your policies; I love my church so much I must hate you for not loving it. I love yogurt, cheese, and butter so much I must hate you for being a vegan. I love my opinions so much I must hate you for having your own.

If people are not going to reflect us back to ourselves—validate both the entire population we claim to represent and ourselves—what good are they? We shalt not have strange goofs before us.

Hatred is a twisting perversion of paradoxes wherein we can claim a love for God so fervent it justifies hating another. Say "hello" to the super idol, raised from the hate we have formed by shaping an idol of prejudice from muddy depths of our love.

A few years ago a university study confirmed the old adage that there is "a thin line between love and hate."[5] It seems the same brain circuitry is involved in feeling both emotions. The major difference is that, with feelings of love, a large part of the cerebral cortex shuts down, along with judgment and reasoning abilities. With hate, much of the cortex remains open.

This makes perfect sense, in a way. We can always give a million reasons to justify our hatreds, but our love? Often we cannot explain our love at all, except as an open and full-hearted mystery, just like the unfathomable mysteries of the God who is love. This study also helps explain why unreasonable love can so often tumble into hate; and why hatred, once engaged by reason, finds it so difficult to break freely into love.

It is that thin, thin line between love and hate that can so confuse our sensibilities and thrust us so far apart from each other. It leaves us convinced that we can make society more loving if they—the backward people who do not understand all things as we do—will just embrace the correct ideas and the idols they lead to.

For the past several decades, offense taking and apology demanding have become recognized, predictable tools of political and social manipulation. They, of course, serve the super idol in much the same way as those hammered-out weapons of rhetoric, re-forged. Offense says, "You are not a tolerant, compassionate person; you are merciless, and may be a kind of *-ist*."

Apology answers, "No, I am tolerant and compassionate; see my mercy! There's no *-ist*! No *-ist*!"

It always fails to convince because deep down we all know that tolerance and compassion and even justice and mercy are either born of a place of fertile love—in which case they are authentic and give rise to more of the same—or they are just words manufactured from a place of sterile intimidation and compulsion. Then they die on the air when uttered. Love cannot be codified and compelled. They must arrive freely, or they are not at all connected to love (and, yes, by the word *love*, I mean God). With no real love, there can be no genuine peace.

So here we are, poised once more at the looking glass, where Humpty Dumpty is choosing the meaning of things. We have taken a long journey into the malleable modern buzzwords of a super idol and tried to reconcile them with something as constant and unchanging as love. We have discovered that moving beyond the established (if insufficient) understanding of God does not work if we actually mean to pursue love. If we try to separate God and love then nothing at all can remain rooted in objective truth, and then only idols reign.

Do we remain here, telling God to eat our dust, imagining we have moved beyond all that stodgy claptrap that came before us and our moment? This moment, we are convinced, is peculiar in its wisdom, as every generation in its own moment has believed of itself. Or do we step back through the glass to a place where we still have a chance of battling back our idols in an effort to access God and love?

CHAPTER TEN

The People of Gods

> *Man is certainly stark-raving mad; he cannot create so much as a flea, yet he creates gods by the dozen.*

MICHEL DE MONTAIGNE

Having volunteered at my parish to take training as a minister of consolation, I was sitting with a family and helping them to plan the liturgy for a Mass of Christian Burial. All of the music, they informed me, was to be from "the old Latin hymns. We don't want any of that modern stuff."

Aware that our parish musicians were not too familiar with older hymns, I assured them "Ave Maria" was pretty standard at funeral liturgies and wondered which other hymns they might have in mind. "Panis Angelicus," I suggested, "for Communion?"

It turned out the family had no idea what "Panis Angelicus" was, knew only "Ave Maria," and were content to leave the remaining hymn selections up to me, "as long as they're in Latin." They wondered, also, if the Mass responses could be in Latin as well. "Pop left the church when they took away the Latin," they explained, "so we think he should have his Latin Mass."

"Well, our Mass is a *Novus Ordo*—the so-called new Mass," I said, "and in the vernacular, but I'm sure pastor would be fine with singing "*Pater Noster*" and the "*Angus Dei.*" Will that do?"

As the saying goes, you'd have thought I was speaking another language. The confused-looking family admitted that they couldn't tell a "*Pater Noster*" from a "*Dona Nobis Pacem*" from a "*Miserere Nobis.*" All they knew was, "Pop stopped going to church when they took away the Latin, and now Mom insists that we have as much Latin at the Mass as we can get."

Part of the Consolation Ministry's mission is to accommodate family requests as much as the parish is able, and to offer sensible, sensitive alternatives where we could not. I tactfully noted that our priests and altar servers lacked training in the old rite, and the family's own unfamiliarity with Latin prayer responses could end up making an undignified travesty of the funeral. "What happens after the sign of peace, when Father intones, "*Agnus Dei*" and no one joins in? Might that not add to Mom's distress? Don't you think the best thing to do is what you *can* do, which is to pray the Mass in your own tongue? Can we stick to the vernacular, while I make sure all the hymns are in Latin?"

It took a long phone call with Mom before an agreement was reached. A few days later, some forty-plus years after his last Mass attendance, Pop entered the church in his casket to the organ strains of "*Ave*

Verum Corpus." The family seemed comfortable and comforted. As the liturgy progressed, though, and the family's unfamiliarity with the order of the Mass kept them looking my way for prompts, I could not help but mourn for the decades of Eucharistic consolation, the sacramental graces and the sense of community that had been lost to this man (and to his family). They sacrificed all to the idol he had made of the Latin Mass. While certainly a powerful and beautiful liturgy, the Latin Mass is not to be accounted as more meaningful than God himself and placed before him.

Given our love for God and Church, we people of faith fall into this trap with surprising, almost terrifying ease. We become enthralled with something specific to our faith, and because the object is a good thing (or a good idea) that is related to our worship, we don't even realize that we've created a strange god. It could be the bible, a nun's habit, or an element of the liturgy that we've put before the true God.

Part of this is, perhaps, a simple byproduct of attempting to balance the horizontal and vertical aspects of faith. The horizontal is the common devotion of the community of faith—the prayers and responses, the lessons and sermons, the recognition of our shared adventure in the engagement with something greater than ourselves. The vertical exchange is the lifting of all of that toward heaven in the act of worship, in faithful assurance that as we reach up to God, he is reaching down to us. This is a living, breathing, real-time lifting high of the cross. The horizontal is the beam of the cross (humanity and church reaching out toward each other), and the vertical is the stationary, heaven-focused post that is so vital, if anyone is to be raised up in Christ, who is at its center.

In Rumer Godden's classic novel, *In This House of Brede*, a newly elected Benedictine abbess leads an arduous Christmas liturgy and then deflects a compliment from one of her nuns by saying, "It wasn't I. . . . *It* is splendid. That is the blessing of the liturgy, it wipes out self."[1] This is very true. Liturgical prayer serves to subsume the individual into the collective community of faith and then join all of those voices on earth to those in heaven, "that all may be one." As such, we might expect liturgical prayer to prove resistant to the creation and elevation of strange gods; but even here, we cannot resist our human habit of attachment, all of which then becomes one more thing that we set between God and ourselves.

A few years ago, I recorded podcasts of Compline (the night prayer before sleep that is part of the Liturgy of the Hours) and all of the mysteries of the Rosary. I invited my blog readers to use these podcasts with their own prayer if they found them helpful. The podcasts seemed well received, but one day I got an e-mail from a man demanding that I remove from the group the Luminous Mysteries (or, Mysteries of Light), which were instituted by Blessed Pope John Paul II in 2002. "They do not belong in there, and you must stop recommending them to people," the man wrote. "The traditional Rosary is the only true Rosary, and those new mysteries are heresy!"

The man ended his missive with a threat that if I did not respond to his concerns, he would find out the name of my bishop and let him know that someone

was messing with his beloved devotional and traditions. I helpfully gave him the name of my bishop, but
I thought about that e-mail for a long time.

The Rosary is a contemplative prayer that I love very
much. When I pray it regularly, my days go better—not
least because it provides fifteen to twenty minutes of
Christ-focused meditation that slows down my breath
and heart rate. A Catholic does well to pray the Rosary
but is not required to do so. The rhythms of the Rosary
are not for everyone. Saint Thérèse of Lisieux lamented
that she could not stay awake for it. As the Rosary is
not part of the Deposit of Faith, Blessed John Paul did
nothing wrong in expanding the meditation. The man
who contacted me loved the Rosary too—or at least
he did once. He now had an idea of the Rosary, and
that idea had become something that could brook no
diversion. That's what happens when our loves become
ideas, and our ideas become idols.

The irony is quite bitter to note. In our day-to-day
lives we are habitually keen to subjugate Almighty God
and the significance of his commandments to suit our
own excuses, rationalizations, times, and purposes; but
we do not like our self-created gods to change. And
within the Church, we the faithful—we the people of
gods—can create some of the most intractable idols of
all.

In an earlier chapter I mentioned a priest who hated
his first meetings at new parishes where, he said, he is
introduced to "the god of this is how we have always
done things." That god has a partner called, "and
these are the people who have always done them." I
do believe these paired godlings exist in most churches

and are not exclusive to Catholic parishes. My evangeli-
cal friends tell stories of ministerial nepotism whereby
the children of people who have overseen particular
ministries for years step into available posts—even small
voluntary ones—making it difficult for other people to
become involved. I used to belong to a parish where
the joke was, if you wanted to get involved in any sort
of lay ministry you had to wait for someone to die or
move, "not just to the next town but out of state." One
of my sons complained of the zealous and unwelcoming
way people guarded their positions. "It's like a bunker
mentality," he said. "They refuse to share responsibility
or to make room for others who might have something
to contribute; their ministry is all wrapped up in who
they are, and it becomes the be all and end all."

The other side of that closed-off mindset—and
quite an equal god of our making—is the open-armed
idol some parishes and churches construct of being
community.

Creating a strong faith community is an essential
goal for any pastoral team, but sometimes the idea can
be allowed to grow into such an unwieldy obsession
that some churchgoers feel harassed if they don't want
to get involved and are always on edge as they await the
next week's surprise. Not too long ago, a priest-friend
recounted helping out at a nearby parish one Sunday. "I
just said the Mass the way I always do, and afterwards I
had people thanking me and saying, 'It was so nice to
just have a Mass, without all the rest of it.' I wondered
what was going on over there."

Being familiar with the parish, I told him: "It's probably the clapping. Everyone gets applauded at every

Mass—the greeters, the altar servers, the musicians, the deacon if he has preached, and the children. They all get acknowledged, and the visitors are encouraged to stand up and be welcomed with applause. And sometimes, to be encouraging, the pastor will invite the congregation to applaud itself for coming to Mass on such a beautiful or miserable day."

The priest looked horrified. "That much applause, all the time? It's so cheap!"

I took his meaning, and it's a conversation I've had with other Christians (not only Catholics). Some like the clapping and others, who argue that volunteers and lay ministers do what they do for love of God, say that "to applaud like that pulls the offering down to earth, doesn't it?" Applauding folks after the hard work of Easter and Christmas, when everyone bears a bigger load, is one thing. They feel that Easter and Christmas are "nice times to thank people for what they do all year, but is it necessary every week?"

After one such discussion, a friend—meaning to underline his point—e-mailed a quotation to me. It's an excerpt from *The Spirit of the Liturgy*, written when the Holy Father was still Cardinal Joseph Ratzinger:

> Wherever applause breaks out in the liturgy because of some human achievement, it is a sure sign that the essence of liturgy has totally disappeared and been replaced by a kind of religious entertainment. . . . Liturgy can only attract people when it looks, not at itself, but at God, when it allows him to enter and act. Then something truly unique happens, beyond competition, and people

> have a sense that more has taken place than
> a recreational activity.[2]

Benedict was specifically addressing applause that had broken out after a penitential rite that included liturgical dance, but his point is worth considering. It is a very fine thing to build a sense of community in a parish, but like anything else, going overboard with that intention can get in the way of the first purpose of church attendance, which is the worship of God. One can argue that the strengthening of community is itself a kind of worship, one where we find God in each other and celebrate his divine spark working amid all of us— and that's certainly a point of view worth pondering. But to me this seems like a secondary, less direct sort of worship that can easily (and unintentionally) end up serving our need for self-worship. Whether it's liturgical dance we're watching, or an over-fussy traditionalism involving one hundred yards of fabric and alb-wearing, episcopal train-carriers, or liturgical pantomime performances, they manage to make many members of the community feel "included." At the same time, these actions can stop the liturgy cold as proud family members break into applause. When we overstuff the liturgy with human trappings, we risk making our worship too much about ourselves and our ideas; and it becomes that much more difficult to lose ourselves to God.

I think, on some level, this is the reason I am happiest at a weekday Mass, where the simple, direct liturgy—usually unencumbered by either ill-conceived creative embellishments or tense, traditionalist precision—draws us so powerfully and mindfully toward Christ.

Of course, even there, in our simplest means of worship, the stuff that goes off inside our heads like popping flashbulbs of self-interest can end up getting in our way, and becoming one constantly rising strange god after another. As much as I would like to say that my own ego-ripe opinions and my inner godlings have never disturbed my worship or affected my prayer at Mass, I would be lying. In fact it shames me to admit that I can bring all of my self-reflective idols with me into Mass, line them up like trophies before the altar, bow to them through the monkey-chatter of my brain, and then pack them up (along with a few newly minted ones) to take home with me.

This has happened to me more times than I'd like to say, but there is good news. Godden's abbess was right; if we can truly submit to the liturgy, it eventually wipes out all of that self-involved thinking and self-adulation. One day I arrived at weekday Mass with a head full of Lizzie concerns, and (oh, it pains me to relate!) there was the priest praying before the Blessed Sacrament before vesting. This was the same priest whose prayerful, mindful-but-slow Mass I had tapped my toe through twice already that week. Shamefully, my interior prattle went something like this:

> Gawd, you're so obnoxious, what is wrong with you? Here you are, getting into the pew before the Blessed Sacrament, and you're whining because you're going to have Mass said by a good priest who might take five minutes longer than someone else. You are hopeless. You should be grateful you even

have a priest. God should have lost his
patience with you a long time ago.

I decided I would pray my chaplet of Divine Mercy
and offer it for the intentions of both my husband and
this priest in atonement for "Bad Lizzie," the difficult
woman they both had to deal with. It went well until a
woman I see every day at Mass—I call her "Babushka
Lady" because she arrives with a tote bag full of prayer
books, wears a babushka, and never speaks a word to
anyone—plopped herself down in the pew directly
before me.

In the middle of my prayer, Bad Lizzie restarted
her interior complaints: "Oh, for crying out loud, are
you kidding me? The church is empty. She has twelve
hundred seats to choose from, and she plops down
directly in front of me. She makes me pull back my
beads and blocks my view. *Woman*!" My harassed better
self moved to the left, mentally gave Bad Lizzie a smack
upside the head, and got back to prayer.

The Mass as has been called "the perfect prayer," and
as it so frequently happens, the day's readings perfectly
answered my anxieties and my arrogances. From the
prophet Daniel:

> We have sinned, been wicked and done evil;
> we have rebelled and departed from your
> commandments and your laws. We have
> not obeyed your servants the prophets, who
> spoke in your name to our kings, our princes,
> our fathers and all the people of the land.
> Justice, O Lord, is on your side. (Dn 9:5-7)

The responsory psalm followed with a plea for
mercy—mercy for nations, mercy for the individual,

mercy even for my bitchy instincts: "Lord, do not deal with us according to our sins."

And then the Gospel! It spoke to me with a graceful directness. It spoke to the innate generosity of my spirit, which is always so at war with the stingy wickedness of my heart:

> Be merciful, just as (also) your Father is merciful. Stop judging and you will not be judged. Stop condemning and you will not be condemned. Forgive and you will be forgiven. Give and gifts will be given to you; a good measure, packed together, shaken down, and overflowing, will be poured into your lap. For the measure with which you measure will in return be measured out to you. (Lk 6:36–38)

The great promise, summed up in a few lines, is applicable to us all. Why do we forget that? If we were not so busy in our bunker mentalities, fussing with the created idols of ministries, our jobs, our responsibilities—the things by which we forge our worldly, earth-bound (and, as my priest-friend might say, our "cheap" identities)—our eyes would be more readily fixed on God. Then we'd become not competing gods but something so much finer: partners with the Almighty. If we can say no to our egos and yes to what is before us, then, in every assent we utter, every stitch we knit, every empty bowl we fill, every lonely life we consent to touch, every hateful remark we respond to with love, we assist in creation—with the continuation of the world. This is just what Mary did when she said

no to her own concerns and questions in order to say
yes to the Holy Spirit.

When we put ourselves and our ideas aside, we work
with the Creator, for whom no need is too small and
for whom love knows no limits. It is the great secret.

And so, that day, with those readings overpowering
my own inner noise, the Mass and Holy Communion
managed to overcome and suppress Bad Lizzie and fill
me with something like awe.

"The blessing of the liturgy is that it wipes out self."

After Mass, the Babushka Lady retreated to a back
row with her bag of prayer books, and, as she often
would, stayed there for a while in silent prayer. I stayed
to pray a Rosary for someone's intention. Off in one
of the corners, a group had gathered to say a Rosary as
well. The group seemed made up of people to whom
life had handed some rough days of suffering, but I was
in my own prayer and paid them no heed until I heard
the clear treble voice of the lone woman among them. I
don't know if she was a patient recovering from a brain
accident or if she had a different issue, but when it came
her turn to lead a decade, she was permitted to do her
imperfect best: "Hail Mary, (unintelligible) Woman!
Bless! You give us Jesus!"

I wondered what my passionate e-mail correspondent would have made of that "nontraditional" Rosary.
Ten times the woman announced it; ten times her col-
leagues prayed the response. No one minded that her
prayer was, on the surface, less than perfect and outside the textbook. They fit the prayer around what she
could contribute and went blithely forward. They fit
the woman into their prayer group, and she became

part of the whole. She was absorbed, subsumed, and indistinguishable from the larger prayer. Community: that all may be one.

I was blessed and humbled to hear the woman and that group as I prayed my isolated prayer in my corner. Her struggles and her boldness to dare speak an "imperfect" prayer, gave huge witness. We are all imperfect. We bring our visible and invisible imperfections into church and—gathered together—our varied selves contribute to the greater whole, just as raindrops, snow, dew, and hail all make the river run. There is no idolatry, then, because in the sublimation of ourselves into this marvelous whole we lose our singular, broken identities. Our broken identities are where the creation of idols begins. The Christ, who has promised to gather all nations to himself, has, in these moments, done precisely that—collected us and drawn us to his light and love; and for a little while we are relieved of the burdens of our own ideas.

There is no need to look elsewhere; there is no need to wander because we are in the place of wonder. "Ideas lead to idols," said Gregory of Nyssa, and "only wonder leads to knowing." And in these moments of collected respite, we arrive at knowing.

Thus are our pretty, distracting gods banished, at least for a time, in those moments when dissimilar people—a gracious and brave lady with halting speech, an oblivious Babushka wearer with many books, and Bad, Bad Lizzie—all come together, like dew and rain, to be joined and disappear in oneness.

> Dew and rain, bless the Lord; praise and exalt
> him above all forever.

> Frost and chill, bless the Lord; praise and
> exalt him above all forever.
> Ice and snow, bless the Lord; praise and exalt
> him above all forever.
> Nights and days, bless the Lord; praise and
> exalt him above all forever.
> Light and darkness, bless the Lord; praise
> and exalt him above all forever.
> Lightnings and clouds, bless the Lord; praise
> and exalt him above all forever. (Dn 3:68-73)

It is the whole world in prayer. It is the whole world in each of us—our dew, our rain, our light and dark, our frost and clouds.

Beyond the idols we create with our egos and ideas, there is an alternative un-earthly universe where we may encounter the deep and constant reality of God. No wonder it scares off so many. In our age the self is everything to be celebrated and never to be diminished. Church subsumes; liturgy subsumes; community subsumes; and when we are subsumed, all of the idols disappear; we become not lone worker bees, but the very buzz of the hive.

And what sweetness is found therein.

My Dreadful Idol

When I first conceived of this book, a friend of mine, who holds degrees in religious studies and philosophy from Columbia and Oxford and is thus a determined agnostic, asked what I thought to call it.

"I'm thinking *Everyday Idolatry*," I said.

"Great title!" he said, enthusing over its rhythms, "and a great topic. You'll be hard pressed to stop at five or ten, though."

He was correct. Once I started pondering the matter, it seemed to me everything in life had the potential to become an idol: anger, past injuries, praise, pride, possessions, politics, patriotism, porn, poetry, film adaptations of Jane Austen novels, human love, family relationships, hate, the fetus, the baby, abortion rights, gay rights, constitutions, careers, reality shows, social media, fitness, food, pets, even religion and its trappings. And, with the exception of the Austen films, almost any of these idols are directly or indirectly spoken against in scripture, because God knows who we are and the depths of our brokenness.

I have seen the phrase, "Nothing human is alien to me," attributed to Michel de Montaigne, Oscar Wilde, and Gandhi; and I have no idea which of them actually said it. In short order it became very clear to me that nothing human is exempt from becoming an idol we will place before God. Any number of human ideas and feelings could be found on any given day to be taking up space between God and us. I would stumble over the burnished little things as I vacuumed or brushed the dog or peeled carrots or read e-mails. If I was busy I would scrawl a note to myself on whatever was handy: "Such and such can become an idol; think about it." Sometimes I would simply snatch a Post-it note, scrawl "idol" across it and slap it on to my computer (for the Internet) or on the dog's collar (because I was crazy about her), or on the bathroom door (for whoever was inside it). My family was amused at first. Then they became worried. "Honey," my husband would call meekly from the kitchen, "can I use these napkins you've been writing on? Or are they still notes?"

Having made a conscious decision to use relevant stories from my own life as illustrative examples of how easily we create our idols, I had not thought to prepare myself for how me-centric the project would become. Once I actually began writing, wondering about idolatry became a kind of idol of me, by me, and for me. While extolling Dorothy Day's penitential-seeming use of instant coffee, I realized that I had half a dozen envelopes of rather expensive and robust gourmet coffee in my freezer and not one but two pricey coffee brewers on my kitchen counter. Egad! Had I made an idol of coffee? Where was my own humility? Did I not love God enough to drink the freeze-dried stuff? But then, God was good, right? Surely, he wouldn't ask it of me!

Maybe it was the coffee, but from time to time I'd find myself growing skittish about it all and my husband would kindly remind me that an idol is, by definition, a strange god placed before the Almighty, and I hadn't done that of the Kenyan Free Trade Extra Bold. *Yet.*

Beyond these false considerations, though, a genuine case of idol building was going on, and in such a slithery, almost imperceptible way.

It is a challenging thing to write a book while working and also running a busy daily blog. Often by the time I was done with a day's work and ready to give some time to the book, I'd find myself with an empty head and brains gone blank. I had a monumental case of writer's block; and for weeks I sat before the flickering screen, staring at the fake white page with no words on it. Like a sad Old Testament prophet, I would sigh and remember the days of yore, when *Commonweal* editor Grant Gallicho would say, "You have a lot of words." He never clarified his meaning, so I won't misrepresent them, but I decided to count on my words. If I had had a lot of words once, I would have them again, God willing. In an effort to stimulate the synapses into firing, I began writing the book out in longhand and then—when I could make sense of it—transcribing what I had written.

Between that time-consuming endeavor and my normal work routine (which I admit is excessive, because I love my jobs), I more or less stopped cooking or marketing for the family. It was "order in," or they were pretty much on their own.

Then, suddenly, I could not find the time to watch a few innings of baseball with one son or return the phone call of the other son.

I could not find the time to write a thank-you note for a thoughtful gift, or invite a friend in for coffee, or ask the in-laws over for lunch. Whenever anyone said, "Would you like to," or "Can we," I would say, "I can't; I can't do anything until I finish this book!"

One discovery I made in the process is that even if you are managing to make it to church on Sunday and squeeze in fifteen minutes of prayer time here or there, if you do not have time for your family and friends—if you're willing to put other things, most notably your work, before them—then it's only a matter of time until you start to put your work before God and create a genuine idol of it.

That was what happened to me. If I was not being all I could be to my family, at least I was still praying as much of the Liturgy of the Hours as I could, every day . . . until I wasn't.

At least I was still praying the Rosary every day . . . until I wasn't.

Well, I was still managing to make the weekly hour of Eucharistic Adoration that has been my constant wellspring of learning and consolation for more than a dozen years . . . until I wasn't.

But Sunday Mass. That was something that I would never miss—not for this! Not for a project that is all about God, a project that I had lain before the cross and completely offered up to him, to grow or die according to his will. And then came that final weekend deadline, when I did miss Mass although, truthfully, not wholly intentionally. It just happened.

But still. There it is. Intentional or not, I had my head so buried in my work that I managed to put it before God and to forget to "keep holy the Lord's day"—a commandment-busting twofer. Thank goodness that upon realizing what I'd done (or hadn't done), I didn't compound the issue by taking the Lord's name in vain. That would be the trifecta but with no worthy payout!

That's not being over-scrupulous (scrupulosity can also be an idol if it is taking your focus off God and placing it neurotically upon yourself). It just is what it is.

So, what you have been reading, and (please God) gleaning something useful from, in these 150 or so pages is the object of my unintended but very real idolatry. It's my strange god and golden calf, this idolatrous book about how easily we create our idols every day.

Dorothy Day said, "I really only love God as much as I love the person I love the least." She was very right. We also love God only as much as we are willing to ponder his good gifts in our lives (yes, we all have them) and feel gratitude. The gratitude expressed every day foments real joy, and it cannot help but move us to praise him. And before praise of the Lord no idol can stand.

We will never live an idol-free life while we live *in corporale*, but we can at least be aware of our common tendency to create idols unintentionally. We can recognize the havoc everyday idolatry can play in our personal lives and our spiritual lives if we do not constantly try to knock the idols aside, before they stand too completely in the way of God's constant and consoling love. He aches for us with a longing that our own yearnings for him cannot begin to approach.

> Believe that he loves you. He wants to help
> you himself in the struggles which you must
> undergo. Believe in his love, his exceeding
> love. He is always there, although you don't
> feel it; he is waiting for you and wants to
> establish a "wonderful communion" with
> you.[1]

About the Cover

The image of a church window, its stained glass replaced by the icons we use daily amid our Internet surfings and with our "smart" gadgetries, was a stroke of genius by the designers at Ave Maria Press, and I invite the reader to play a little game with the cover: look closely within this lovely window and see if you can identify the icons relevant to certain idols we've discussed in the book.

Then, see if you can spot a few that may be more personal to your own life.

This "game" could be a useful exercise from time-to-time, a starting point for contemplating where one's focus has become an over-focus; where indulgence has become over-indulgence until—because of our penchants for everyday idolatry—something has been placed between oneself and God.

One way to keep our balance amid all of the icons and idols is to recall that the genuine Icons of our religious traditions have very little in common with our app icons or idols:

- An Icon looks out from an Intrinsic light and points to its Source; there are no shadows in which to hide.
- An idol looks out from man-created light and points to itself; invites us into the shadows.
- An Icon teaches us how to focus, how to quiet down, collect ourselves, and hear the small, still voice.
- An idol throws noise, images, and issues at us, non-stop, scatters our thinking, and deafens us to any voice but its own.
- An Icon whispers wisdom.
- An idol shouts soundbites and mindless trendspeak.
- An Icon inspires us to chant to the Most High.
- An idol inspires us to chant to it, and to ourselves.
- An Icon looks us straight in the eyes and dares us to pursue truth.
- An idol wears shades and tells us what we want to hear.

Special thanks to Ave Maria Press's Tom Grady, Bob Hamma, and Karey Circosta, and most especially Kristen Hornyak Bonelli and John Carson, for their responsiveness and thoughtful input regarding the cover. When working with a team is as pleasurable as this has been, it deserves mentioning.

Notes

Introduction

1. *Hardball with Chris Matthews*, MSNBC, June 5, 2009.
2. Evan Thomas, "The Perils of Punditry," *Newsweek*, June 22, 2009, Vol. 153, No. 25.
3. Bill Carter, "Want Obama in a Punch Line? First, Find a Joke," *New York Times*, July 15, 2008.
4. John Fund, "The Hunt for Sarah October," *Wall Street Journal*, September 9, 2008.
5. Elizabeth Scalia, "Uncredentialed Wonder," *First Things*, January 25, 2011, www.firstthings.com/onthesquare/2011/01/uncredentialed-wonder.

Chapter One: God before Us

1. Simon Jacobson, "Honoring Parents Who Don't Seem to Deserve Honor," Meaningful Life Center, January 30, 2000.

Chapter Two: God after Us: The Idol of I

1. Benedict XVI, "We Never Fall From God's Embrace," February 15, 2012, www.news.va/en/news/pope-we-never-fall-from-gods-embrace.
2. G. K. Chesterton, *Orthodoxy* (Hollywood, FL: Simon & Brown, 2012), 51.
3. Benedict of Nursia, *The Rule of Saint Benedict*, Translated by Leonard J. Doyle (Collegeville, MN: Liturgical Press, 2001).
4. *The Breakfast Club*, Directed by John Hughes. (Hollywood, CA: Universal Pictures, A&M Films. 1985).

Chapter Three: The Idol of the Idea

1. Cardinal Joseph Ratzinger, *Co-Workers of the Truth: Meditations for Every Day of the Year*, (San Francisco: Ignatius Press, 1992), 377.

Chapter Four: The Idol of Prosperity

1. *The Rule of Saint Benedict* (Collegeville, MN: Liturgical Press, 2001).
2. Ibid.
3. Dan Wooding, "The Day Mother Teresa Told Me, 'Your Poverty Is Greater Than Ours,'" *Assist News Service*, July 4, 2010, www.assistnews.net/ Stories/2010/s10070019.htm.
4. Fyodor Dostoyevsky, *The Brothers Karamazov*, translated by Richard Peavar and Larissa Voloknonsky (New York: Farrar, Straus, and Giroux, 2002), 313.
5. Louette Harding, "Sing Out Sisters," October 9, 2010, *Mail Online*, www.daily-mail.co.uk/home/you/article-1317969/

The-Benedictine-nuns-Abbaye-Notre-Dame-lAnnon-
ciation-How-recorded-album-confines-isolated-abbey.
html.

6. Jim Forest, "What I Learned about Justice from
Dorothy Day," *Salt of the Earth*, http://salt.claretian-
pubs.org/issues/DorothyDay/learned.html.

7. Ibid.

Chapter Five: The Idol of Technology

1. Thomas Merton, *Contemplation in a World of
Action*, Second Edition, Restored and Corrected (Notre
Dame, IN: University of Notre Dame Press, 1999).

2. Benedict XVI, "Pope Asks Bloggers to
Give Internet a Soul," Vatican Radio, April 24,
2010, http://storico.radiovaticana.va/en1/
storico/2010-04/374892_pope_asks_bloggers_to_
give_internet_a_soul.html.

3. "Casting Wide in the Net: An Interview with
Brandon Vogt" by Elizabeth Scalia, Patheos.com,
http://www.patheos.com/Resources/Additional-
Resources/Casting-Wide-in-the-Net-Elizabeth-Sca-
lia-10-01-2011.html, October 1, 2011.

4. Benedict XVI, "Message for the 44th World
Communications Day," Vatican website, http://
www.vatican.va/holy_father/benedict_xvi//
messages/communications/documents/hf_
ben-xvi_mes_20100124_44th-world-communications-
day_en.html, May 16, 2010.

Chapter Six: The Idols of Coolness and Sex

1. John Irving, *The World According to Garp*, (New
York: Modern Library, 1998), 207.

2. Paul VI, *Humanae Vitae*, Encyclical Letter on the Regulation of Birth, Vatican website, July 25, 1968, www. vatican.va/holy_father/paul_vi/encyclicals/documents/ hf_p-vi_enc_25071968_humanae-vitae_en.html.

3. "Dementia patients in care homes 'should be allowed to have sex as it denies them a basic human right,'" *Mail Online*, June 26, 2012, www.dailymail. co.uk/news/article-2164767/Dementia-patients-care-homes-allowed-sex-denies-basic-human-right.html.

4. Paul VI, *Humanae Vitae*, sec. 17.

5. Rachel Jones, Jacqueline E. Darroch, Stanley K. Henshaw, "Contraception Use Among U.S. Women Having Abortions in 2000–2001," *Guttmacher*, November/December, 2002, www.guttmacher.org/ pubs/journals/3429402.html.

6. Elizabeth Scalia, "Marriage: Not a Right, but an Office," *First Things*, May 15, 2012, www.firstthings.com/ onthesquare/2012/05/marriage-not-a-right-but-an-office/ elizabeth-scalia.

7. Jane Fonda, Robin Morgan, Gloria Steinem, "FCC Should Clear Limbaugh from Airwaves," CNN, March 12, 2012, www.cnn.com/2012/03/10/opin-ion/fonda-morgan-steinem-limbaugh/index.html.

Chapter Seven: The Idol of Plans

1. William Blake, "Several Questions Answered," in *The Complete Poetry and Prose of William Blake*, (New York: Anchor Books, 1997), 474.

Chapter Eight: The Super Idols

1. Martin Luther King Jr., "The Drum Major Instinct," delivered at Ebenezer Baptist Church, Atlanta, Georgia, February 4, 1968.

2. Annie Lamott, *Bird by Bird: Some Instructions on Writing and Life* (New York: Pantheon Books, 1994), 22.

3. "Anne Rice Quits Christianity—But Not Christ," *Baltimore Sun*, July 30, 2010, http://weblogs.baltimoresun.com/news/faith/2010/07/anne_rice_christian.html.

4. Abraham Lincoln, "Second Annual Message to Congress," December 1, 1862. *The American Presidency Project*, http://www.presidency.ucsb.edu/ws/index.php?pid=29503, accessed November 5, 2012.

5. Benedict XVI, "Angelus Address," Vatican website, July 10, 2011, www.vatican.va/holy_father/benedict_xvi/angelus/2011/documents/hf_ben-xvi_ang_20110710_en.html.

Chapter Nine: Through the Looking Glass: Super Idols and Language

1. G. K. Chesterton, "Negative and Positive Morality," *Illustrated London News*, January 3, 1920.

2. Ratzinger, *Co-Workers of the Truth*, 377.

3. John Allen Jr., "Forgiveness as the Catholic Yoga: An Interview with Robert Enright," *National Catholic Reporter*, February 28, 2011, http://ncronline.org/blogs/ncr-today/forgiveness-catholic-yoga.

4. Elizabeth Scalia, "The Hate That Feels Like Love," *First Things*, March 1, 2011, www.firstthings.com/

onthesquare/2011/03/the-hate-that-feels-like-love/
elizabeth-scalia.

5. Steve Connor, "Scientists Prove It Really Is a Thin
Line Between Love and Hate," the *Independent*, October 29, 2008, www.independent.co.uk/news/science/
scientists-prove-it-really-is-a-thin-line-between-love-
and-hate-976901.html.

Chapter Ten: The People of Gods

1. Rumer Godden, *In This House of Brede*, (Chicago:
Loyola Classics, Reissue Edition, 2005), 197.

2. Cardinal Joseph Ratzinger, *The Spirit of the Liturgy*, (San Francisco, Ignatius Press, 2000), 198–99.

Conclusion: My Dreadful Idol

1. Bl. Elizabeth of the Trinity.

ELIZABETH SCALIA is a Benedictine Oblate and managing editor of the Catholic channel at *Patheos*, where she blogs as the Anchoress. She is also a columnist at *First Things* and for *The Catholic Answer*. Scalia was a featured speaker at the Vatican's much-noted 2011 meeting with bloggers from around the world and has a multimedia presence that includes contributions to NPR and *CBS News Online*, and a stint as a regular panelist on the Brooklyn-diocese-produced current events program *In the Arena*, seen at NETNY. net. She is the author of *Caring for the Dying with the Help of your Catholic Faith*, was a contributor to *Disorientation: How to Go to College Without Losing Your Mind*, and has been involved with the editing of both religious and secular books, most notably, *Why We Hate Us: American Discontent in the New Millennium*.

Founded in 1865, Ave Maria Press,
a ministry of the Congregation of
Holy Cross, is a Catholic publishing
company that serves the spiritual and
formative needs of the Church and its
schools, institutions, and ministers;
Christian individuals and families; and
others seeking spiritual nourishment.

For a complete listing of titles from

Ave Maria Press

Sorin Books

Forest of Peace

Christian Classics

visit www.avemariapress.com

ave maria press® / Notre Dame, IN 46556
A Ministry of the United States Province of Holy Cross